Chapter 1: Sweet Jilly Muffin

My parents did not believe in magic. The
either. But they recognized the powe
magicians, they knew precisely when to

The sound of Mom inserting a casset
enough to summon us all to attention. '
touch of the play button. We'd listen. We'd close our jaws, plant our
feet on the ground, and keep our eyes on Mom. We would be entirely
under her control, restrained by the three-second silence before the
music began, ready for whatever came next.

Sometimes there was a violin and a keyboard. Sometimes there's a
roaring chorus of voices. Drums may occasionally be heard, but only
when accompanying a marching band. It would be years before I had
the words to adequately characterise and explain the limited types of
music we were permitted to listen to—a cappella hymns, southern
gospel, and certain classical pieces such as Handel's Water Music. I
was an adult by the time I realised why these, and only these, were
the kind of music permitted in the Duggar home. But, in that steamy
living room, I had no need for words. The music alone was plenty.

I enjoyed it most when Mom played "Ever in Joyful Song!" Almost
soon, the violin began marching, whirling, and twisting like a kite
caught in a storm. All of us Duggars would get caught up in it, from
my oldest brother, Josh, to whichever infant was old enough to rock
on all fours, dripping with excitement.

At times, music was a distraction. Mom used it as a tool to get us out
of a bad mood or to infuse some joy when needed. She'd also use it
as a motivation to keep us focused while we folded clothes or
unloaded groceries. Whatever her purpose for clicking the play
button, she made good use of it. Music had power, and it was just as
easy to turn off as it was to put on. Especially if someone said the D-
word.

Most of the time, the music would resume and we'd be able to
continue. However, if someone's pleasure jumping became too
violent, it was either Handel's Water Music or game over: quiet.
Most of us Duggar kids knew the rules, but when friends came over,

we had to stop because one of them was sticking their buttocks out, or worse, shaking it.

By the end of the presentation, there was no more jumping.

Dancing was forbidden, so I learnt to hunt from an early age.

We lived in Springdale, Arkansas, a city of around 70,000 people at the foothills of the Ozark Mountains, in a small house on three quarters of an acre adjacent to a church. There were cow fields all around us, and because we were homeschooled, we spent a lot of time outside, breathing in the fresh, northwestern Arkansas air. But I didn't hunt with a gun or set traps. Rather than rabbit or quail, I was looking for acceptance. And by the time I was old enough to support a baby on my hip while folding laundry—which I believe was around seven or eight years old—I was hands down the finest approval hunter in the entire Duggar clan.

When it came to receiving a nod of acknowledgement or appreciation from Mom or Pops at the dinner table, or, best of all, being singled out for direct praise for listening intently while sitting perfectly quiet and perfectly still on one of the mauve-pink living room chairs during family Bible time at the end of the day, I worked hard to stand out as the most mature child in the room. When the tape player was switched on and we were jumping for excitement, I always made sure to keep my movements modest and my hopping straight. There was no wiggle in my buttocks, and there was no possibility of the music being shut off on my account.

"Stop, guys!" Pops might recall when it was Bible time and Joy was performing somersaults on the floor, and the twins—either set—were fighting for the best seat on the couch. "You resemble a can of worms! Look at Jill. She has her notebook and Bible out and is ready to go.

I wanted to be a decent girl. I strived to be a perfect daughter. And my desire to be good and perfect even won me a unique pet moniker that only my parents used. I was Sweet Jilly Muffin, the family's fourth born and second daughter. "Oh yeah," Pops would respond anytime he was asked about his children and he assumed none of us were paying attention, "Jill's so sweet, so kind, and compassionate. She looks the most like Michelle of all of my daughters."

Jill Duggar

Biography

Breaking Free and Finding Herself

Chase Hunter Long

TABLE OF CONTENT

I was overjoyed when my parents implemented what became known as the buddy system. Each of us older kids was assigned a younger sibling to assist with feeding, dressing, and bathing, as well as to sit next to and buckle up in our fifteen-passenger van when we travelled anywhere. I was the first to sign up and acquire my own friend, and I enjoyed caring for my little sister Joy from the time she was about a year old, and then my brother James when he arrived. I was a ten-year-old girl whose parents entrusted her with their precious children. I felt like a little mother. I could not have been happier.

Mom was the most incredible teacher. Whether it was creating flaky pie crusts for Pops' favourite pumpkin pies or learning how to curl my hair perfectly, I enjoyed the opportunity to learn from her. Spending time with Mom made me really pleased, and an invitation to accompany her on a one-on-one outing to conduct errands—which frequently meant staying out much past bedtime—left me beaming for days.

Mom was also a role model. She always put us kids first and would wake up around the clock to care for us if we were unwell. Even when she was sick, she'd stay awake all night, prescribing medications, passing out Popsicles, and giving us damp towels to relieve our fevers. She showed me what it is to be a mother through both the good and bad times.

All I had to do to get my parents' approval was behave how Mom and Pops anticipated. From sunup to sundown, the Duggars reminded us youngsters of those expectations and restrictions. Mom homeschooled us during the day, and Pops finished each evening by sitting in the living room or in the hallway between the girls' and boys' bedrooms and reading from the Bible while discussing character, sin, and everything else that mattered in life.

As a child, I never saw my parents as oppressive or controlling. Instead, in my youthful perspective, they were as loving, fun, and amazing as any girl could ask for. At the end of each day, they'd write us notes, confirming and encouraging us for whatever we'd done well that day—being kind to a sister, working hard on our homework, going above and beyond to help out. I never felt the need to challenge their rules, and neither of my parents were restrictive or confining. If anything, I was grateful for the boundaries they established for our family. Even though I knew my parents were strong and capable of protecting us, I was aware that there was more to life than the acreage we lived on or Pops' used car business. They repeatedly reminded us that the world was full of risks, temptations, and traps. My parents' protection was only so effective out there.

"Be careful, girls! Let us be modest! Keep your dress down or tucked into your pantaloons.

Pops didn't have to tell us frequently, but when we went on a bike trip, one of my younger sisters would need to be reminded. Whenever it happened, I checked myself as a matter of routine. Many of us would. We understood how vital modesty was. Nobody wants to be accused of being "revealing."

As girls, Mom created practically all of our clothing, and we exclusively wore full-length skirts or dresses. All of the dress fabric made cycling difficult, so Mom sewed us all full-length pantaloons to wear underneath. I enjoyed my parents' watchful eyes as they scrutinised us for modesty. As I grew older, I became increasingly concerned that I might be immodest and cause someone to have negative thoughts.

It was much more difficult to maintain modesty the first time we visited a beach. We visited family in Savannah, Georgia, and went to the beach one day. It was hot, and even though I was eight or nine years old, I had never seen the ocean, tasted salty air, or felt sand between my toes before. My initial steps were cautious, like an astronaut on a strange planet, but I loved it right away.

But I was also disturbed.

That excursion to the beach was the first time I saw so many individuals wearing swimming suits in public. Even though my parents had taken us to the quietest section of the quietest beach, I could see individuals in the distance wearing what appeared to be almost nothing—a few couples and a large number of families. I tried not to gaze so that no negative ideas would enter my mind. But it was difficult not to, and I worried for Pops and my brothers. We girls had been reminded again how much more difficult it was for boys to keep their minds pure. I couldn't fathom the battles they were having out on the sand.

Still, the beach was a new experience for all of us kids, and it also revealed a different side of my parents. They were soon swept up in the excitement of the moment, cheering on the children as they ran, tumbled, and played tag with the waves. We were all having a good time playing in the shallow water, and I, like my parents, became a little lost in the moment.

The magic broke when I noticed someone approaching us. A girl my age was going straight toward us, surfing the little waves on her boogie board.

"Why are you wearing those clothes to swim?" she asked, getting close enough to look at us. "Why are you not wearing bathing suits?"

"Uh, well," I responded, stuck between the anxiety of telling a falsehood and the awkwardness of talking to someone who was only wearing underpants in public. "We didn't plan on coming here so we didn't bring anything else with us."

The girl stared at me for a long time. She took in my long dress with its now-sandy hem and my blouse with sleeves that nearly reached my elbows. I tried to avoid looking at her beautiful skin. I focused my attention on the waves instead.

I was relieved when the questions stopped and she hurried back to the waves.

Instead of having to keep any of this a secret, I was pleased that my parents allowed me to tell them whatever I saw or heard while I was away. It was evident that they had carefully considered how they intended to raise us, and they always made time for a talk about the distinctions between our family and others—even if they pursued different techniques.

My parents liked to use role-playing to help us prepare for life.

Mom's teaching style reflected who she was—a housewife and full-time mother who knew how to patiently nurture her children. Pops participated in the role-playing games as well, although his approach was slightly different. He spoke like a teacher or preacher, using pictures to emphasise his point, but he also had the charisma of a politician and salesperson. When it was his turn to shape us into the young men and women he envisioned, he piqued our interest by breaking down the tasks ahead of us into easy, binary options.

His lessons had an impact on me. They also worked on my siblings, since whenever Pops spoke to us in this way—his voice a mix of tenderness and warning—the entire room fell silent. There were several short sermons and stories, but one stood out above the rest.

"I was about twelve or thirteen when I went to a seminar," Pops once told us. "That was the first time I heard about the power of music and the risks of rock and roll. It's not only the lyrics, but also the music. When the drums start playing, the backbeat has so much influence over us. It is capable of exerting power over us. When I got home that night, I realised the music I'd been listening to wasn't Christ-honouring because it was essentially rock music with Christian lyrics. I felt so convicted that I grabbed my eight tracks and smashed them with a hammer.

I had no idea what an eight track was until Pops explained it to me, and I had only ever heard rock music during a parade or a fair. At the time, I had very little exposure to contemporary Christian music. But I was attracted by the picture of Pops, who was just a few years older than me, discarding his whole music collection because he wanted to follow God's instructions in his life and live like a Christian should—set aside with convictions. He had claimed that I was similar to my mother, but there were many aspects of my father that I admired as well.

The story became a kind of legend in our house, and Pops told it frequently. We appreciated that it was both practical and inspiring, and that we could apply it in our own lives. We liked the notion of Dad wielding a hammer against the devil, and we liked it because it signalled the beginning of our family's relationship with a man named Bill Gothard, who had delivered the lecture that had had such an impact on Pops. Gothard was the founder and leader of IBLP (the Institute in Basic Life Principles), and as film crews and enthusiastic whispers and stares from fans became a regular occurrence, Pops' relationship with Gothard and his organisation grew in importance. And becoming more difficult.

But before we were on TV, life was simpler for the Duggars. We put the principles Mom and Dad were teaching us into practice, and we came up with our own ways to emulate our parents. For a while, all of us older kids and our friends formed various organisations, such as the What Would Jesus Do Club, where a group of my sisters and a few friends would get together to make WWJD bracelets and discuss handing them out to others. Another group was formed, and all of us girls read and discussed the book Beautiful Girlhood. My sister Jana also started an ice cream-eating club in the shed. I visited all of them frequently, especially Jana's.

These clubs were enjoyable, but the one I really wanted to attend would not let me in. And it bothered me.

One evening during Bible study, Pops informed us that the local gas station had begun selling pornography. We were all startled and upset, and my elder brothers, Josh and John, were resolved to do something about it. They invited Steffan and Jeremiah, two of their other homeschool pals, and founded the Boys Christian Outreach Team, or Boycott Club for short. Their objective was clear: they planned to buy a large number of Christian tracts (little leaflets explaining how to become a Christian), distribute them across town, and urge everyone they knew to boycott the gas station. And if that wasn't enough, there was a rumour that every time they met, they would eat pickles with Josh's homemade seasoning salt—a legendary recipe that Josh created himself using Lawry's seasoned salt, onion powder, lemon pepper, salt, pepper, and a few other secret ingredients.

The Boycott Club was where it was at, and I was eager to join. But no matter how much I begged or how gently I asked, my application was turned down because I am a girl. It wasn't until I gave two dollars to join that the boys agreed to bend the rules slightly for me.

It was the middle to late 1990s. I was only a child at the time, too young to be assigned Joy as a buddy, but my recollections are vivid. We left early in the morning from our home in northwest Arkansas, driving down Interstate 40 via Little Rock and all the way across Tennessee to Knoxville. It was a long trip, but as we got to our destination, we knew it was worthwhile.

We were attending a conference in the University of Tennessee's basketball arena, and the venue alone made my eyes pop. The bleachers rose high and broad, brilliant lights shone on the stage, and a men's quartet practised as people ran around onstage putting the blue drapes and green ferns in position. We located and occupied a row way up high in the back. Mom had given us each a bag containing a colouring book, a new box of crayons, and some munchies. Despite how exciting the bag was, I was too preoccupied with looking.

Everywhere I looked, I saw people who were just like us. Families with identically dressed children—girls in matching floral blouses and floor-length skirts, males in navy or khaki pants and button-down shirts. Parents marshalling their family groupings around the arena, some with four or five children, others with nearly twenty. After spending the early years of my life being taught how different we were from others, it was almost astonishing to see so many people dressed like the Duggar family.

As the ceremony began, I was captivated by the music. The four sang in perfect unison, and the entire audience was then led through a succession of joyful hymns—"We're Marching to Zion," "Leaning on the Everlasting Arms," and "Victory in Jesus"—all accompanied by a single, skilled pianist.

Despite his impassioned advocacy for the significance of children and large families, he remained unmarried. He had never married and had no children, yet I never heard anyone at any of the conferences complain about it. Mr. Gothard was unlike the rest of us. The customary norms did not appear to apply to him.

He loves quoting scripture. Because the King James Version was the only translation utilised, the language was outdated and dusty. But it was powerful and authoritative, and I listened closely, appreciative of the Bible's clear precepts.

"Lo, children are a heritage of the LORD: and the fruit of the womb is his reward" (Psalm 127:3).

"The woman shall not wear that which pertaineth unto a man, nor shall a man put on a woman's garment: for all that do so are abominations unto the LORD thy God" (Deuteronomy 22:30).

"In like manner also, that women adorn themselves in modest apparel, with shamefacedness and sobriety; not with braided hair, or gold, or pearls, or costly array" (1 verse 9 of 2 Timothy).

I was young, so I probably only understood a fraction of what I heard—and when Mr. Gothard started talking about "the seven basic principles of design, authority, responsibility, suffering, ownership, freedom, and success," I zoned out—but many of the words that echoed around the arena had been said many times by my parents at home. And judging by the expressions on the audience's faces, whatever Mr. Gothard was saying had to be worth listening to.

When the next group of folks were brought up, I didn't need an explanation. It was a family, with a finely dressed father leading a perfectly dressed mother and eight perfectly dressed children following closely behind. They all grinned as they glided gracefully and elegantly across the platform, forming a perfect semicircle in front of the microphone. Mr. Gothard briefly interviewed the father about how his business was doing and how his family was such a blessing before stepping back as the family began to sing.

Each of the eight children was smiling serenely as they sang.

The harmony was nothing short of superb.

This, I subsequently found out, was an IBLP tradition, and they were a Model Family.

Watching the family sing and then hearing the acclaim when they completed made it evident that the Duggars fell short of the perfection required to become a Model Family. When we played our instruments at home, the sound was occasionally difficult to hear. We didn't follow the strict "early to bed, early to rise" schedule that we were advised was necessary for success. We could almost get everyone dressed the same, but it wouldn't be long until someone spilled, smudged, or dribbled all over their clothes. We were not Model Family material. Not yet, at least.

The IBLP conference in Knoxville signalled the start of a new chapter in my life. Previously, my world had been small. We were like settlers in a new and hostile land. My life was almost totally spent at home, where we were educated, entertained, and taught how to live. The house was little, but it was a place of protection. It was our rock, and I knew every detail of it. The areas beyond it were vast and unknown, filled with unseen perils that lurked like quicksand.

But that trip east changed my perspective. We were not alone in this world. There were others like us out there, folks who looked, sang, and dressed similarly. For the short days we were there, I was able to let my guard down a little, which I appreciated. Mr. Gothard and the IBLP had brought us together. He'd taken us home.

I was overjoyed that our first visit to Knoxville was not our last. The annual conference became a regular feature on our family calendar, and we began attending other, smaller IBLP activities throughout the year. These trips helped me understand what it meant to live according to Mr. Gothard's ideals. My parents initially did not send us to any children's groups, primarily because the groups were expensive, but also because they desired to have us with them so we could fully benefit from the education. I would sit and take detailed notes on the significance of avoiding alcohol and adhering to my parents' authority at all ages, including after marriage. Each seminar would conclude with a call for attendees to raise their hands as a demonstration of their commitment to following whatever IBLP principle had just been discussed. I felt pressured to demonstrate my devotion to God, therefore it wasn't long before my hand was raised in the air.

I wasn't the only one taking note or comparing myself to what I observed. One evening, not long after my first homeschool conference, one of the Model Families came to our area, and a local church hosted a small gathering of homeschool families to hear them speak. The family sang and played music before the parents discussed their daily routine and shared parenting advice. At one point, the mother described a new notion that she had begun teaching her younger children.

I looked at my parents. They both listened closely.

In the days after the incident, my parents had us test out the new notion at Bible time, role-playing yes, ma'am/yes, sir, I'd be delighted! We quickly became accustomed to the habit and made it our own.

The IBLP was not the only expansion in our planet at the time. My father began to get active in politics, successfully standing for state legislature in 1998. Whenever it was in session, our entire family would relocate for four months to a leased home just outside of Little Rock, Arkansas. Homeschooling would continue as usual, but instead of gathering around the kitchen table or learning outside in the remote northwest of the state, some of us older, more mature children would be allowed to bring all of our study materials to the capitol building while Pops worked. We'd attend small committee meetings or sit in a corner of the balcony area while Pops worked on the floor below. We weren't the only ones doing it; there were even a few homeschooling families whose fathers sat on the floor while their children studied on the balcony.

We picked up on some of the politics, but I really liked chatting quietly with my buddies while eating candy and other special delicacies provided by Pops' coworkers. However, my brother Josh was interested. When the session was finished, he'd dress up in a suit and tie and go downstairs. We'd see him swagger alongside Pops, a twelve-year-old politician in the making, shaking hands and discussing whatever bill had just been passed. They referred to him as the "Little Governor."

"Nike!"

That code word became as potent as the sound of a tape player in a house full of Duggar kids. However, while pressing the play button sent us into a whirl of vertical motion, "Nike!" had the opposite effect. When it was called out, everyone instinctively stared at their feet. Nobody hesitated. Especially not the boys.

For as long as I can remember, my parents have cautioned us about the dangers of sin. They told us that sin may take various forms, such as lying, stealing, disobeying our parents, or being a tattletale (which my parents described as "stirring up contention among the brethren"). But probably the most harmful and damaging sins of them were those involving sex and temptation.

When we were younger, the lessons were simpler and more straightforward.

It began one summer when I was around nine, Josh was twelve, and the twins, John-David and Jana, were ten. It must have been around the time of the Spice Girls or Britney Spears—neither of whom we had ever heard of—and whenever we walked into town, it seemed like every other lady we encountered was wearing outfits that exposed all of their curves and the majority of their tummies.

We initially attempted to ignore it, but with so many others following the fashion, it was nearly impossible. One of my older siblings finally broke down one day as we were leaving a gas station.

"Don't look!" they exclaimed as we passed a particularly barely dressed teenage girl. "There's a bad girl dressed immodestly over there!"

Mom quickly turned around and looked at each of us in turn. She was not smiling.

"Children, be mindful of how you speak about people and the language you use. I want you to protect your eyes, but I also want you to avoid thinking negatively about other individuals who wear a certain way. When you encounter someone dressed immodestly, it is acceptable to urge your siblings not to look, but do not disparage the other person. That girl simply doesn't know any better. It is not our place to make judgments. "We should be praying for her instead."

She paused briefly. "Before becoming a Christian, I used to maintain my lawn while wearing a bikini. I honestly didn't know any better."

The quiet that fell over us all was as heavy as a deep winter snow. It was difficult to understand why Mom was dressed so improperly while Pops was ruining his music collection in the name of holiness. But Mom was the most Godly woman I knew. Thinking about her metamorphosis made me love and appreciate her even more.

Mom continued the subject again that evening, during Bible study at home. "You know what made me want to stop dressing the way I used to?" It was when I discovered from your father that males are not the same as women. When women wear tight or exposing clothing that exposes certain areas of their flesh between their collarbone and knees, it catches guys' attention and can arouse sensual cravings. It can cause individuals to think negatively. When girls do this to guys, they are deceiving them. That is not good, because it can lead to sin."

I suppose that was the first time I heard the word defraud, and it stuck with me for a while. I didn't want to instil dirty thoughts in young guys, and I vowed never to swindle them, no matter how I looked or behaved. I would be pure and Christlike, even if it was tough at times. Perhaps someday I will be worthy of a truly godly man.

Around that time, the phrase "Nike!" became part of the Duggar code. My parents were seeking a means to keep the boys from having dirty thoughts, but they needed something more powerful than ordering them not to look whenever temptation approached. "Nike!" was their solution. Whenever we were out and saw a girl dressed badly—someone deceiving guys by maybe putting negative thoughts in their minds—someone would cry "Nike!" and everyone would immediately lock their gaze on their shoes until the all clear was given.

But Nike wasn't sufficient.

Later that night, as we snuggled into our beds for Bible study, Pops appeared sad.

"I am so sorry," he said, addressing us all but staring especially at the lads. "You shouldn't have had to see that." I was wrong to bring us there tonight. We will not attend that church gathering again.

For a while, Bible study revolved around the idea of how difficult it may be to do things correctly, even in Christian communities. Not all Christians held themselves to the same standards. "Sometimes," remarked Pops, "you have to be bold and learn to stand alone."

This must have started Mom and Pops thinking about Temple Baptist, because they announced shortly after that we were leaving to join a new church founded by a pastor and homeschool father. Pops allowed the church to gather in a trailer house that he owned, and it immediately reminded me of the ATI and IBLP conferences.

I can't remember how I felt about us leaving Temple Baptist. Some of that time in my life is fuzzy, and the recollections are out of focus. But I recall Pops and Mom calling me into their bedroom and closing the door. I was eleven at the time, and they both appeared pale and exhausted in ways I hadn't seen before. I wondered if Mom had cried.

"Hey," Pops said gently. For once, the words were not flowing quickly and effortlessly. He had to look for them, hunt them down. "Josh... has been speaking with us." He has admitted to several things he has done. Can we speak with you about it?

I nodded. Sat quietly. And waited.

I waited for Pops to find the next words he was going to say.

Chapter 2: "A Window of Opportunity that God has Given Us"

When Josh left, we didn't talk much. The issue of what had happened to Josh was not embargoed or off-limits; it was simply not something I wanted to discuss, so there wasn't much to say. Mom and Pops told us only the most basic information about Josh, so all I knew was that he'd been sent away to stay with some of their friends, that he'd be working construction, and that hoped he'd be back soon. That was all. I was relieved to go on and put everything behind me.

In addition to "Nike!" and all the other helpful expressions that guided our steps, we had grown up being continuously warned not to "stir up contention among the brethren." It was a technique for our parents to restrain us siblings from talking negatively about each other or bringing anyone down, but it eventually evolved into something more sinister. By prohibiting us from discussing anything contentious or sensitive with one another, the admonition not to "stir up contention among the brethren" becomes an instrument for silence, control, and guilt.

Despite their ambiguity concerning Josh, my parents rarely missed an opportunity to involve us in other aspects of life. Whenever there was labour to be done around the house, from daily tasks to maintenance and yard work, we were each assigned a duty, some tools, and a clear set of instructions. Josh and John had both learned to drive before the age of twelve, and by the time I was that age, I could teach my younger sister to read, change diapers, babysit for short periods of time, and prepare supper for the entire family, as well as any adult.

It was no different with Pops' political aspirations. When he campaigned for state representative, we joined his campaign team. He gathered an army of Duggars and drove us over northwest Arkansas, posting yard signs and handing out brochures at events. We'd stop at Wendy's on the way home, and even when the days were long and the waiting was lengthy, it felt good to be involved, especially when he won his first term and then re-election. As children, we had a purpose. We weren't trapped in a classroom, exposed to all the dangers of public education. We were out in the real world, assisting Mom and Pops to serve God within it.

That sense of purpose got even stronger when Pops announced that he had decided to compete against the incumbent for the Republican nomination to the US Senate.

"I have never sought election to the United States Senate. "I don't want to run," he stated one day. "But I genuinely believe God wants me to do this. I prayed about it and did something I only do for the most important decisions in life."

One of my siblings posed the question that we were all contemplating.

"What, Pops?"

"I flipped a coin three times," he added, his eyes widening and a smile of delight spreading across his lips. "All three times, it landed on heads. So I said, 'Okay, God, you want me to run, so I will run.'"

I was about eleven years old at the time and knew little about politics or the difficulties of running against an incumbent, but I was aware that senators and their families lived in Washington, DC. I didn't want to leave Arkansas and our friends, but I understood that sacrifice was an important part of serving God.

"Ministry sometimes requires sacrifice," Mom and Pops would say frequently, before going on to quote Psalm 34:19: "Many are the afflictions of the righteous: but the Lord delivereth him out of them all."

So we travelled the entire state, putting up yard signs, passing out pamphlets, and eating Wendy's on the way home. The days and distances covered were significantly longer than Pops' prior state campaigns, and the sacrifice felt genuine. And when primary election day arrived, and we all dressed in matching clothing and accompanied Pops to the polling place—where a small group of media had gathered to tell the story—I was confident that a God-given win was just around the corner.

I was mistaken.

Pops lost.

His response was calm and measured. He reminded us that God never told him he would win, only that he should run. He was content that he had followed God's call, and I admired him for it. I also believe that not having to relocate to Washington, DC for several years was a relief for us kids.

However, the loss did not mark the end of the saga. In truth, that was only the beginning of everything. One of the journalists that questioned Pops at the polling station was from the New York Times. He'd written about a crazy Christian person with a bunch of kids who lost at the polls. The tale had appeared in print, along with a photograph of my parents and the fifteen of us Duggars lined up in a row, marching into the polling location, smiling joyfully at the photographer in our handcrafted, matching costumes.

A week or two later, Pops received a call from a magazine that wanted to learn more about our family and publish a profile on us. Pops was unsure at first, and he explained that our family was going through a difficult time, with their eldest son temporarily gone and all. But Dad and Mom prayed about it, and then he informed the rest of us that he wanted us to pray together to see if God was opening up a new opportunity for our family. We did what was asked, and we all agreed that it was what God wanted us to do. We didn't have much choice in the issue.

After the story was released—complete with a photo shoot of all of us (except Josh) in a field somewhere, surrounded by hay bales—Pops left a message on our answering machine from a man who said he was from Discovery Health and wanted to produce a one-time documentary about our family. Pops was sceptical.

"I don't want you to make us out to be freaks," he stated when he called the person back.

I couldn't hear the other side of the conversation, but Pops appeared serious as I listened and for a long time afterward. He appeared to do so anytime he was paying close attention to Mr. Gothard or another member of the state house of representatives.

"You know," Pops told us later during Bible time, "when I ran for Senate, I didn't understand God's ultimate purpose in it. But, after reading the article and watching the TV show, I'm beginning to believe that God had something greater and better in store for us. This is an opportunity that God has given us to demonstrate what a Christian family may be like. This is our time to show the world that children truly are a blessing from the Lord."

I didn't realise it at the time, and neither did anyone else, but that phrase—"a window of opportunity"—would become as common in the Duggar household as a newborn baby's cries or a director's request for silence on set. Mom and Pops would say those five words all the time, and "a window of opportunity" became part of our family jargon, much like "Nike!" It was an instant explanation of why some decisions were made, a reminder of the blessings received and the sacrifices that we must all make in return. However, as time passed and circumstances changed, the meaning of those five words shifted. When I heard someone talk about how the initial decision to install TV cameras in our home was a window of opportunity, all I could think about was secrets and lies.

I was grating cheese when the film crew arrived.

"Just act normal," a man with an earring advised me, as a camera loomed in front of my face and a woman in slacks began instructing everyone in my family on what to do. I was twelve now, a bundle of self-conscious anxieties and red-faced discomfort. Acting normally was not an option. I attempted to relax, pulling out my best Sweet Jilly Muffin smile for the camera.

"Look over there, sweetheart. "Do not look at the camera!"

It wasn't easy to appear natural, especially when they made us all line up in our pyjamas outside the restroom door. They wanted to show viewers that we all shared the house's two bathrooms, but it made me feel humiliated, uncomfortable, and a little scared. I couldn't express any of this to my parents. After all, this was a divinely provided opportunity. The greatest thing I could do was suppress my emotions.

It wasn't entirely horrible. At one point, the woman in pants declared that the TV crew would be following us to the shop for groceries. As we pulled our five shopping carts around Aldi, I overheard a murmur that the staff would be paying for everything. So, for the first time, Mom wasn't telling us to stock up on canned beans, ramen noodles, and 48-cent frozen beef and bean burritos. Instead, we were able to load our trolleys with boxes of Lucky Charms and Honeycomb cereals, ice cream sandwiches, frozen pizzas, and all-beef chimichangas. Our trolleys were heavier than ever, and all of us Duggar kids were wearing the same double-wide smile. For once, the upcoming week would not include tater tot casserole or bean sandwiches.

The TV crew came for two or three days the first time, and then returned for a few more days every two or three months. It was a long, gradual process, and we hardly noticed them when they were with us. We missed them when they went, and our weekly meal returned to its customary basics of beans, tuna, and macaroni.

By the end of 14 Children and Pregnant Again!, Josh had moved back in with us. His head had been shaved, perhaps in an attempt to chastise him or instil some humility. I wasn't worried about him, however. I was a kid, and I believed that things would improve now that Josh had been "fixed." Besides, it seemed good to be whole as a family again, especially after Mom gave birth to Jackson, the fifteenth Duggar child. Pregnancy was difficult for Mom, especially during the first trimester when the nausea was severe, but we enjoyed the excitement that surrounds a new baby. To have another sibling to adore and care for made me very pleased.

For a while, the baby dominated the filming. We had been sent a DVD to approve the forty-five-minute documentary, but we still didn't have a television in the house, so by the time the show aired, I'd forgotten about it.

That did not last long.

14 Children and Pregnant Again! became Discovery Health's number one show at the time. Pops was ecstatic.

"We prayed about it as a family," Pops said at Bible time one night, his eyes sparkling with joy. "We felt like God wanted us to share with the world the message that children are a blessing from the Lord, and it's now the channel's number one show! God is blessed with it! God is using us to spread his word throughout the world."

We didn't stop talking about a window of opportunity after that. We now had a new word for what we were doing: "ministry."

The Duggar family continued to grow, and by the time Mom gave birth to Johannah, her sixteenth child, TV crews were frequent visitors to our small home surrounded by cow meadows. It was getting crowded in there, with only two bathrooms and three bedrooms, so Pops acquired some acreage near Tontitown and began the lengthy process of building us a brand-new, seven-thousand-square-foot steel-framed home. I was too young to wonder where the money came from, and I was content with the thought of having a bit of extra space at home. We moved into a rental while the new house was being built, and in true Duggar fashion, we did as much of the labour as possible, including laying the radiant heat flooring, tiling the floors, and much more. Even though we were able to devote a significant amount of time to the project and had a large team, the house was larger. We were still working on a project that we had believed would be completed in a year when Mom informed us that she was expecting her seventeenth child.

The birth of another Duggar imposed a deadline, but our expanding number was not the only reason to expedite our job. A second documentary showed us starting work on the house, but the producers wanted the third Duggar TV special to show us finishing the work and moving in. Thanks to some solid haggling from Pops, the network decided to open the chequebook.

If we were excited about getting free Honeycomb cereal, frozen pizzas, and chimichangas, this took it to a whole other level. A crew of labourers arrived at the location, and the producers flew in an interior designer from New York. She assisted us in selecting bedroom sets and other items that we could not have afforded on our own. There was still a lot of work to be done, but seeing the Big House (as we usually called it) sprinting toward the finish line was worth all of the hard hours.

I'm not sure when I first heard Pops refer to us as "a filming family," but it made sense to me. We studied as a family, worked as a family, and accomplished everything together. I was grateful that Mom and Pops did not have any hobbies outside of us. They were loyal to one another and to us. We were a family that did everything, so why not allow the cameras in and show the world?

There was a fourth documentary, which accompanied us on a road trip, and a fifth, which covered Jennifer's birth as the seventeenth Duggar child. As a "filming family," we were opening our home to the public. By this point, I was sixteen and no longer blushed whenever the camera came near me. The group was almost like family to me, and I was ready to go anywhere they told me. This was our window of opportunity. This was our ministry.

So when Mom and Pops informed us that the network, TLC, wanted to transition from one-off documentaries to an actual reality program about us, I wasn't surprised. It was just another confirmation that this was all a God-given chance. To my mind, it had nothing to do with our desire to be famous or see ourselves on television. After all, we still didn't have a television in the house, and we'd only see rough clips of each documentary when they arrived on DVD. I was dimly aware of when the episodes were broadcast, and people would occasionally compliment us on something they had watched on television. But when Pops asked us to pray about whether we should accept TLC's offer, the possibility of being famous was the last thing on my mind, especially after he revealed the agreement he had made with the network.

"I informed them that our faith is at the heart of our life and cannot be edited out. They said it was our narrative and we could tell it how we wanted."

In the culture of IBLP, it was never acceptable to express pride in anything or anyone, no matter how godly the person or the moral decision. Even though I knew Proverbs 11:2 and 16:18 by heart ("When pride cometh, then comes shame," and "Pride goeth before destruction, and a haughty spirit before a fall"), I was proud of Pops for telling TLC that our faith was unbreakable. I believed in what we were doing and prayed that God would guide my parents as they negotiated.

"They're calling it '17 Kids and Counting,'" he stated one day, allowing the words to linger in the air as we heard the title for the first time. "This is a ministry opportunity that God has provided us. We'd be pleased if it ended tomorrow."

I looked around at my siblings. Nobody disagreed. I got the impression that we were all on the same page. We fully trusted Mom and Pops. Whatever happened to the show, no matter how long it ran, I was confident it could only be a wonderful thing.

I was sixteen when the separate documentaries were transformed into a reality television series, and I was old enough to observe the various pressures placed on our family. The first five documentaries were filmed over nearly three years, but we shot the entire first season of 17 Kids and Counting—all 10 episodes—in a matter of months. The team would arrive three days a week, filming three hours in the morning and another two in the afternoon or evening, sometimes more, sometimes less, depending on the week. Once all of the Duggar family video had been shot, we'd do a series of interviews in a local studio and narrate the show. It went on for weeks, and homeschooling was frequently stopped so that we could go out of the house and film something new and different for the show, such as a trip to New York City for sightseeing or a drive up to Ohio for a family reunion. These events were thrilling, revealing the world to us. Nobody complained, and I suppose we just accepted it when Bible times expanded to include more than just praying and reading the Bible together, with Pops and Mom reminding us of upcoming filming commitments and warning us not to tell anyone about what we were doing. We were now a filming family, and we needed to take it seriously.

Aside from the filming excursions, the new show brought back the traditional privileges we had experienced when 14 Children and Pregnant Again! was filmed. If we went to Aldi during the weeks we were filming, we could load our carts without thinking about the price. On days when the crew was with us, they would bring in food from wherever we desired. Pops even gave us older kids a debit card so that if we were out running errands or driving the younger kids to a music lesson or dental appointment and it was late in the day, we could stop for lunch on the way home and give him the receipt. It was a lot better than it used to be, with us driving around with a Crock-Pot of chilli to feed the kids on the go.

When the first season premiered, we were already in the middle of filming the second. We did not always see them live, as we did with the documentaries, but instead carefully reviewed the numerous preliminary edits that were supplied to us. They hadn't cut out allusions to our faith, as Pops had told them, and when the show aired, I was pleased at the prospect of all those people throughout America watching and possibly being inspired to live for Christ by seeing Christian ideals acted out on a secular television channel.

It wasn't just random individuals who were observing us and taking notes on how we lived. One day, we were informed that we would shortly be hosting a special visitor for lunch. A team of IBLP leaders from Romania was touring the United States, accompanied by several of the top leaders, including Mr. Gothard himself. They were going to be in the neighbourhood and pay us a visit for lunch.

The thrill was immediate. Then came the challenge. The Romanian delegation included roughly fifty members, with about as many US IBLP officials accompanying them. The Big House featured two kitchens, one regular-sized and the other a full commercial one with an industrial dishwasher and super-wide ovens, so we had the ability to cook for large groups but lacked the pans needed to prepare lunch for over one hundred people. Mom sent out a call to her church friends, and a tiny army of spouses and their children arrived to help clean, cook, and prepare for this enormous occasion.

There was no shooting that day, but I doubt we would have spotted them. When we heard the buses pull off the road and roll down our gravel drive, we all took our positions in front. We practised our family greeting a few times and lined up in age order, ready to offer a hand as we flashed our brightest IBLP smiles and introduced ourselves.

We had occasionally rehearsed this at Bible time over the years, especially for the youngest children to learn the drill, and it had always gone well. With the Romanians, however, we encountered some difficulty. Both men and women among them wanted more than simply to shake our hands; they wanted to kiss each of us on both sides of our faces. Aside from handshakes and side hugs at church, dental examinations, and sick visits to the doctor, kids in the Duggar household were not supposed to have much physical contact with the opposing gender. Even though the welcome line was long and awkward—all of us older kids blushed—we accepted it as a cultural distinction. Furthermore, the presence of Mr. Gothard was enough to push any shame to the sidelines.

I wasn't startled by his diminutive stature; I'd seen him up close before, but I'd never seen him outside of a conference, especially in Arkansas, where we live. Having Mr. Gothard visit us at the Big House was a major occasion. In my opinion, having such a man of God visit our home was more spectacular than being met by a fan at an airport, and even more impressive than a visit from the president himself. Mr. Gothard was different from a noisy politician, but he had a comparable attraction. At a little more than seventy years old, with black dyed hair, a round face, and a big smile, he had a twinkle in his eye as he addressed each person directly. His voice was quiet and had a strong northern accent, and he gave each of us a hearty handshake as he carefully proceeded down the line. As he approached, greeting my parents first, then my youngest siblings, I could feel my nerves tighten.

When it was finally my turn, I extended my hand and blurted out the words I'd been practising for days.

"If it weren't for you, Mr. Gothard, I likely wouldn't be here!"

He seemed intrigued. His smile became even bigger. I stammered.

"My parents have always said that they would have stopped having children once they had their twins, numbers two and three. I'm number four, so thank you for teaching them that children are truly a blessing from the Lord!"

I don't recall what he said in response, but I do know how I felt, and it wasn't humiliation or awkwardness. Mr. Gothard was a legend in my eyes, as well as the eyes of everyone I knew. Just having his attention on me for a few seconds made me feel amazing. As Sweet Jilly Muffin, approval seeker, it was a memory I would cherish for the rest of my life.

The Duggar family's favourite meal of tater tot casserole and sauteed green beans (from a cookbook written by the Voellers, one of the most well-known Model Families) must have been a hit, for we were asked to a slew of IBLP events after that. My parents were sometimes called to speak, and we occasionally received free housing and admission to children's activities that we couldn't previously afford. We were becoming a model family. I was invited, along with three of my sisters, to one of their Journey to the Heart camps in Michigan. We were invited to serve as leaders, which was an unexpected honour for me. Even more shocking was that, following the camp, Mr. Gothard personally invited my elder sister Jana to visit IBLP headquarters in Chicago and work there for a while. We were new to the inner workings of IBLP, but we knew enough to understand why only Jana had been invited. She was the only older Duggar girl who was blond, and everyone knew Mr. Gothard adored blonde girls. We'd joke about Jana becoming one of "Gothard's Girls." that never occurred to me how odd, dangerous, and unwise that was. And even if I had, I doubt I could have spoken out against it. Sweet Jilly Muffin had grown up, but I remained scared of conflict and would do anything to avoid it.

I was sixteen years old on the day that several of the church families visited the Big House. It was one of those hot summer afternoons where you couldn't stop sweating, especially since we were all wearing full-length skirts. I'd outgrown the pantaloons a few years ago when I stopped climbing trees and learnt to keep my skirt down at all times, but I felt awful for some of the little kids who were getting grumpy in the heat. So I gained permission from my parents to organise a water balloon fight.

It was enjoyable, and everyone was having a fantastic time shrieking and yelling as we raced each other over the grass. But suddenly a voice I couldn't recognize cried out.

"Stop! "What are you doing?!"

I froze, holding a large tub of water balloons. I turned to see one of the fathers, red-faced from more than just the heat. He was upset that his children were playing like this without his permission, and veins appeared above the buttoned-up collar of his shirt. He was yelling at the top of his lungs, signalling for his thirteen children to rush toward him. They all obeyed immediately.

"Who granted you permission to do this? Please answer me! "Who allowed this?"

Nobody responded, and he kept ranting. In the midst of the turmoil, I sneaked away, running to the farthest end of the house and locking myself inside the bathroom. It must have taken me ten or twenty minutes for my heart rate to return to normal, and at least an hour before I felt bold enough to unlock the door. I guess I got my avoidance of conflict from Mom. I doubt it came from Pops. When the show was just getting started and we were settling into our new lives as a filmmaking family, something very unexpected happened. Something made Pops agitated in ways I hadn't seen before.

It began with a letter.

Josh had been courting a girl about the time we left the church that allowed immodest dancing at its Christmas service, long before he was expelled. He must have vaguely admitted to her about the abuse he had committed, since I later learned that the girl had sent a letter to him, expressing her outrage at what he'd done. But instead of sending it to him, she slipped it into a book.

Four years later, in 2006, a friend at church borrowed the book, and the letter reappeared. It was read by someone we knew, who went to the same church as us. Instead of speaking with Mom or Pops, she sought additional information from church leadership, called a hotline, and told DHS of what she believed to be a possibly abusive scenario.

Everything changed while we were in Chicago recording with Oprah and then attending our first IBLP Headquarters Christmas party. Pops received a call informing him about the inquiry, and as soon as the trip ended, I, the majority of my sisters, and my parents were all interviewed. We attended a closed-court session. Strangers would visit our house at various hours to ensure that the doors were locked and that everyone was sleeping where they should be.

That was terrifying.

I was afraid I would say the wrong thing and someone would take us away from Mom and Pops. One incorrect word, one stupid answer, and I'll be the one to split our family apart.

I tried not to exhibit my fear and buried it deep inside. But I was older now, and the stakes were higher—it touched all of us. So it was more difficult to hide the dread produced by the investigation than the fear caused by the abuse that DHS was investigating.

Mom and Pops took the time to sit with us all, pray with us, and explain as best they could what was happening. I appreciated it, particularly their counsel.

"Just tell the truth," they both said several times. "It's a safe environment, and they're simply doing their job. Tell the truth, and everything will turn out well."

I was wrapped up in my own terror, but not so tight that I didn't detect how Pops was feeling.

He was angry.

I had heard that the individual who discovered the letter and called the hotline had also spoken with a few others at our church. While the specifics remained secret, the news of my brother's issues went around our small hometown church. Some families greeted us with kindness and compassion, but I feel others were jealous of our success with the television show and viewed us with distrust. "They threw us to the wolves," Pops claimed when the probe was over. "They did not advocate for us at all. They are the ones who made this happen. They are the ones that authorised DHS to conduct an investigation into our family, despite the fact that we had already resolved it."

The fallout was massive. We weren't sure who we could trust, who was on our side or against us. We distanced ourselves from the church and no longer allowed them to have services at the Big House. It caused a major schism inside our church, and I believe the church eventually separated.

Like Pops, I was upset and angry.

But after it was finished, all I wanted to do was put it behind me. I was frightened of losing my family and deeply disturbed by the questions I was forced to answer. I wanted to forget about it. I just wanted to get away from it all as soon as possible.

Chapter 3: Clipped Wings and Hills to Die On

I sat up straight, straightened my skirt again, and readied my brightest grin. A quick scan left and right revealed that Jana, Jessa, and Jinger were all doing the same. It was one of our first public appearances since the March 2014 publishing of our book Growing Up Duggar, which is about our life and religion. I was sceptical at first, but it turned out to be much easier than I had anticipated. Pops had taken care of everything, from the writer who assisted us with the language to dealing with the publisher. He also told us that because of the advance, he was able to purchase some new, lightly used harps for us.

Writing was new to me, but talking came naturally. So, during an impromptu Q&A in a North Carolina bookstore, we all knew what to expect. We were aware of the unwritten screenplay we needed to follow.

"How do your children feel about the show? "Do you like it?"

"Oh, it's a family ministry," Jana replied. "You know, sometimes it's hard, but the film crew is like family to us."

"We love having them in our home," I said, hoping to remove any negative connotations from my sister's response.

"And how long do you think it's gonna go?"

"Well, I don't know about that," says Jessa, "but I do know that we just feel like it's a window of opportunity that God has given our family."

"And we'd be happy if it was over tomorrow," Jinger stated. "We're just leaving it up to God."

It was all correct, but it was not the complete truth. Even in the early days, my feelings were not as straightforward as the script we were following. Season one has been a hit. Seasons two and three, which premiered shortly after, aired a total of forty-eight episodes in 2009. With all of our success, the filming that was now taking place for ten or eleven months of the year began to set the rhythm of our life.

The benefits were still good. We got to travel more—Mom and Pops went to San Francisco for their 25th wedding anniversary, and a group of us flew down to El Salvador on a mission trip. However, some of the most memorable experiences were the basic ones, such as a road trip to Washington, D.C. or Branson, Missouri, and Silver Dollar City. We'd squeeze into our old RV, open the rear window, and play a game of getting semi drivers to hoot at us. We'd sleep in a Walmart parking lot at night and then stock up on Little Debbie oatmeal cream pies, deli chicken tenders, and potato wedge fries when the store opened the next morning.

I adored the moments we spent together, especially when it was just the Duggars. The presence of the film team provided many benefits, but I rapidly developed a hatred for the way they liked to surprise us. I suppose it made for good TV to see us react in real time to the news of whatever challenge or adventure they'd planned for us, even if it was only an escape room or a trip to the park, but it came to the point where I was stressed almost every time they filmed. I was either attempting to hide my uneasiness and worry when they surprised us, or I was pretending to be happy while we were filming something we had already rehearsed. I needed to keep my reality away from the television.

We began to receive some unfavourable attention as the show's popularity grew. We had a family blog where people could contact us, and at first, Pops performed all of the screening of emails, warning us not to read anything that came through it. He also warned us about any criticism we could encounter online or hear about elsewhere, telling us that "People will say terrible things. Naysayers will always exist.

We didn't have much internet connection back then, and there was a soft rule that we couldn't use social media until we got married. But, while Pops could manage the majority of the emails, the volume of real mail that people sent to our house began to build up. Some of us females began to help filter through it all and answer to folks as soon as possible. Most of the time, the letter was overwhelmingly encouraging and friendly, but occasionally we received something bad. It could be a letter with condom packets inside, an all-caps message imploring us to STOP HAVING KIDS BECAUSE

YOU'RE OVERPOPULATING THE EARTH, or plain old hate mail telling us we were terrible people. Our parents would always answer with the same advice: "When you do the right thing, you will always face persecution. Don't forget that Jesus was persecuted and never sinned in his entire life.

Their comments comforted me. Despite the fact that I was programmed to seek approval like a sunflower scanning the sky, these negative responses did not disturb me too much. Rather than being crushed by them, I felt encouraged. I'd been told my entire life that ministry is fraught with difficulties, that following God invariably leads to pain. So, in some respects, the negative feedback was a source of relief. After visiting El Salvador and witnessing the conditions that Indigenous Christians were facing—no electricity, no running water, constant humid heat, and no air conditioning—and frequently hearing from missionaries in other places who lived in similar, if not worse, conditions, I began to believe that the ministry to which God had called us Duggars was far less difficult than others. Seeing the hate mail as a minor sort of persecution for the sake of Christ helped to assuage my guilt. It helped me feel slightly better about things.

I believe that the show's success influenced how the IBLP leaders perceived us. We were still a lot less polished than the other Model Families, but the fact that we were on practically every week of the year made us appealing in other ways. Rather than training and sustaining Mr. Gothard's existing followers, we introduced millions of new people to the world of IBLP. It did not go unnoticed, and in addition to inviting us girls to assist out at camps or volunteer at the main offices, the leaders began to seek Pops' input on decisions.

Pops was pleased to comply. He'd tell us kids about how he'd chatted with Mr. Gothard about this or that, or how he'd suggested a particular person speak at a conference. He appeared to love his new position, but he wasn't only speaking with Mr. Gothard and the other leaders. Pops frequently extended support to parents. Many times, I'd heard him talk to couples about their children, offering advice like, "You need to train them to understand why they believe what they believe," or "The Bible says to 'train up a child in the way he should go: and when he is old, he will not depart from it.'" "We as parents are accountable to God for how we raise our children." Pops was never afraid to tell the truth, even when it stung a little.

Pops agreed with the way IBLP saw the world. Those "seven basic principles" that were at the heart of everything made sense to him and affected the way he and Mom raised us. Mr. Gothard's instruction influenced how little music we could listen to, the cut of our clothes, and the length of our hair. We would be homeschooled and rarely allowed to spend time with anyone other than our parents, elder siblings, or—on rare occasions—church friends. We would never drink, dance, or use contraception after we married.

"Children are a blessing from God" was a basic concept that grounded much of what the IBLP taught, as was the theme of power, particularly parental authority over their children. "Honour thy father and mother; (which is the first commandment with promise;) that it may be well with thee, and thou mayest live long on the earth" (Ephesians 6:2-3) was a commonly taught or cited passage of scripture. Even in maturity, honouring parents was so important that disobeying them was considered a sin. If you wanted to marry but your parents refused to give you their blessing, IBLP doctrine was on their side.

There wasn't much discussion about hell or damnation, but terror was a potent force in IBLP. TV, public schools, and even modern Christian radio stations with their rock music were all threats that tried to keep us from living righteous Christian lives. Children needed to be safeguarded from them all, therefore there was a lot of discussion about "umbrellas of protection"—one of the most important pillars of IBLP instruction. If a child disobeys their parents' instructions or acts in a way that dishonours them, they endanger themselves. Disobeying their parents would mean leaving the safety net, and horrible things may happen. They would face God's judgement if they gave in to sin.

In the universe of IBLP, a parent's authority did not terminate when their child turned eighteen, or even when they married. They continued to discuss the Bible's teaching of "leave and cleave," as well as how couples should make decisions together, but it appeared that they did not truly accept it when it contradicted the teaching of parental authority. It may vary or appear different, but parental control has never stopped or lessened. Like all of my siblings, I knew I would always seek to honour and obey my parents, even when I married and had children of my own. Saying no, going against Mom or Pop's desires, was not something I could ever envision myself doing, especially given our opinions were similar in most areas. My parents had repeatedly promised us that one day we would marry and do things differently than they had. "That's okay," they'd said, and so I assumed that when the time came, if my husband and I made different options than the way I was raised, those judgments would be honoured.

However, even though I didn't see it at the time, IBLP urged parents to clip their children's wings. They taught youngsters to stay with their parents until marriage, and that instead of attending college, children should stay at home and learn other safer trades for labour. They encouraged fathers to start their own enterprises and employ their sons. It was an obvious technique to keep full-grown, adult offspring trapped in the status of dependent youngsters. It seemed like a wonderful plan to my younger self at the time. I had no intention of leaving home or starting a life on my own. Why should I? The world was hazardous and filled with peril. Everything was safe at home, in the Big House, where my parents could protect me.

But no matter how hard Pops tried to keep our wings clipped or how tightly he huddled us beneath his own personal canopy of safety, there was one child he couldn't keep from making mistakes. It was Josh. He got into problems again a few years after being sent away the first time. He'd been caught looking at pornography on someone else's phone while working. Those seven essential principles had little to say about secular therapy or rehab, so Josh packed his bags once more, and Pops sent him away from home for many months to perform some strenuous physical labour in the company of good Christian people and get himself back on track.

And, like previously, we didn't talk about it much.

Josh's troubles were barely mentioned faintly, if at all, but Pops was happy to address almost all of our questions regarding the play (save those concerning money). He would explain our daily obligations, forthcoming events, and frequently encourage us by sharing great feedback he received from others. It left me in no doubt that God was using the show to minister to the nations. Pops would say yes to practically any favourable shooting opportunity that presented itself, and we even had crews from all over the world visit Tontitown to film with us for their own specials. I recall one time when a crew from South Korea arrived. They were really nice, but they had a considerably more gruelling schedule than we were used to, recording five days in a row from seven in the morning until 10, and occasionally eleven at night. I don't recall much about the Russians other than that they were more laid-back and spent time explaining to us how their prior idea to address their dropping birth rate was to give people refrigerators in exchange for having children.

With each season of the TLC show and each one-time program that Pops signed us up for, I could watch him progress. He had sold his old used-car lot and vehicle towing service when he entered politics, but he kept his auto dealer's licence and enjoyed attending car auctions. He rented some land to Josh for use as a car lot, and Pops would occasionally put some of his own automobiles on Josh's lot to sell. As the show expanded, Pops became more interested in buying real estate and protecting what he had, but when he talked about the show and the tremendous influence he believed it was making, he came alive.

"I've always had this great desire to reach people for Christ," he said one day shortly after returning from a trip to New York City, where he and Mom, Jessa, Jinger, and Jordyn—the newborn eighteenth Duggar—appeared on The View. "As we flew over the city, I wondered how we would reach out to so many people for Christ. And then it dawned on me that there were so many people watching the show. We are reaching millions. I never imagined that God would give our family such power over all these individuals."

I shared his surprise that we'd landed up in this situation. It was wild and insane that a family like ours from northwest Arkansas would end up like this just five years after the first documentary, and it was even more wild and crazy that we had done nothing to make it happen in the beginning. The only plausible explanation was that God had opened the doors for us. He'd made a way. This show, as a filming family, was his calling in our lives. For now, at least.

The New York City story became one of Pops' favourites. I saw him say that a lot, especially when he seemed to want to assist someone understand that we weren't in it for the perks or the celebrity, or when he needed to explain that the show found us rather than us hunting for it. Pops, the consummate salesperson, always seemed to know how to pitch his story, and it always worked. At least, everything seemed to work until the one time it didn't.

I heard about it some weeks later. A young man who was a family acquaintance was supposedly talking with Pops one day at the Big House. Pops had been attempting to get the person to participate in some filming, talking about how he believed God was using the show to influence so many people, implying that the numbers reached by our show on television had a greater impact than many other ministries.

"Think about how many people we are able to reach through the show!" Pops had continued. "We regularly reach out to people who would never go to church, but they invite us into their living rooms every week! It's a tremendous opportunity that God has placed right in front of us, and we must be good stewards of it!"

"That's very interesting, Mr. Duggar," the man remarked, carefully selecting his words. "But, you know, Jesus also had one-on-one conversations with people. I believe that is still very essential today."

Pops was apparently frustrated by the resistance, so he attempted a fresh approach and example.

"Just picture yourself in a stadium, and someone gives you a microphone." He let his words hang in the air for just a moment longer than necessary, as if the concept was so grand and glorious that it required more time to process. "You can speak with everyone in the stadium and tell them about the Lord. You'd jump at that opportunity, wouldn't you? It's a no-brainer, right?

The guy shuffled nervously, wondering if telling the truth to power was worth it. He chose the truth.

"I'm not sure, Mr. Duggar, sir. Not if God had commanded me to go talk to the individual under the bleachers. If I knew the Lord wanted me to go talk to one person instead of thousands, I'd have to comply."

Pops froze. He looked like he had just swallowed a fishbone. "Uh-uh," he muttered after he had recovered, shaking his head. "No way." "God would never command you to do that."

When I heard the account, I was startled.

Was Pops truly saying that he believed it was always God's wish for people to be involved in the ministry that reached the most people? And was he telling our friend that he understood God's plan for this guy's life, which involved filming? Was he truly stating that in order to trust God's timing, we must be able to witness the effects within our lifetime?

This was counter to what Pops had always taught us as kids. We'd grown up hearing him say, "Little is much when God is in it," and, "We don't always see how God is working." However, Pops' statements contradict biblical accounts in which Jesus separated from vast crowds to address or minister to a single person. It left me feeling confused and depressed.

Long before our family friend questioned Pops in that way, I had virtually concluded that it would be easier to ignore the whole relationship issue for as long as possible. There were many rules, as there are in many IBLP families (though we didn't call them that). My parents preferred "standards," "convictions," or "guidelines") and had high expectations for how we Duggar children would choose a marriage match. Instead of dating, we discussed courtship, which was far more serious than merely messing around and having fun with others. We were only going to court someone we saw as a prospective marriage partner, and we would always be chaperoned until the wedding day. We wouldn't kiss or spend time alone with each other until we were married, wouldn't say "I love you" until we were officially courting, and wouldn't hold hands until we were engaged. Only a guy could ask a lady to start dating, but if Pops (not Mom) wanted to support what he saw as a good match between a guy and one of his daughters, it was fine for him to drop clues and recommend we get to know one another.

Josh had gotten married at the age of twenty, and I hoped that my Prince Charming would come along soon. But I knew I shouldn't let marriage dominate my thoughts. I also knew my parents loved me and wanted the best for me, so Mom and Pops would never plan our marriages or compel us to marry someone. However, without our parents' approval, no romance could ever begin. Years of IBLP instruction had taught us that no good Christian child should consider defying their parents' desires. The number one prerequisite for a prospective partner was parental approval. Without that, the game was done before it ever began.

We were advised not to simply sit about waiting for our future mate to appear, but to spend our time in ways that distracted us from continual thoughts of marriage. Mr. Gothard even taught that it was desirable to make a vow of single service, pledging to serve God for a set number of years while single. His message was persuasive, but I chose to commit to serving God, my family, and others until God brought my future husband along. I dressed modestly, but inside I was a typical girl who enjoyed romance and love just like everyone else. I had wants and emotions, but I attempted to control them and avoid discussing boys with my sisters. When we were younger, we were all encouraged to tell our parents that we liked someone and ask them to pray with us about it.

I was fine with waiting. As the show progressed from season to season, my life became increasingly full. Not only did I have three young friends to care for—Joy, James, and Jenni—but I was also studying to be a midwife. Between filming, studying, attending births, making sure my three companions were dressed, showered, fed, doing their schoolwork, and everything else, it wasn't too difficult to get my mind off of finding Mr. Right. Besides, Pops was already doing part of the thinking for me.

By the time we finished filming season six, the show had grown so successful that my parents were constantly getting calls for speaking engagements, meetings, and interviews. Because of all of this attention, Pops' opinion and guidance became highly respected and sought after by many individuals. He routinely got calls from people seeking his advice. Sometimes the calls were confidential, but other times dad would allow a couple of us kids to join him as he put the caller on speakerphone so we could listen in and hear them provide an update on their mission.

One morning, before the film crew arrived, I was getting ready in the girls' bedroom with a few of my sisters when Pops walked in, midway through a phone call. He muted it and quickly said, "There's a young man I've been speaking with. His name is Derick, and he is a missionary in Nepal. "Why don't you guys listen in for a while?"

I listened for a while with my sisters, but I didn't want to appear overly engaged. Furthermore, I had things to run, so I didn't pay much attention.

The same scenario happened about a month later, with Pops entering the room I was in and declaring that he was on another call with the missionary guy, and we listened to the chat on speakerphone without saying anything. This time, as Pops got off the phone, he said that Derick had a blog that we should check out sometime. Something about the way Pops stared at me while he talked suggested that he had a plan here.

Thinking Pops was trying to set me up, I naturally avoided expressing any genuine interest. On the one hand, I was twenty-one years old and had no desire to have my father fix me up with any random guy. In my perspective, that would be awkward and strange. Then again, I respected Pops, and there was a small part of me that thought it was nice that he was watching out for me in this way. So I decided to play along, listening intently to what this missionary in Nepal had to say but giving Pops no cause to assume I was interested.

Derick's life was different from mine. He was about my age, only a few years older, and from the same part of Arkansas as me, but while my days were spent with siblings, chores, and TV crews, he had already graduated from college and was serving on the mission field in Nepal. He described some of the things he'd been doing since he and Pops last spoke—visiting remote Himalayan villages, building relationships with people who had probably never heard the gospel before—which sounded adventurous and exciting, especially since I'd been dreaming of going overseas and working full-time in mission work since my first out-of-country, short-term mission trip to Central America.

I wasn't going to get carried away, however. When I next had some free time, I did some research on my own and discovered Derick's blog and Facebook page. There were plenty of excellent images and updates on his efforts, and he appeared to be a decent guy. But I was not interested. I was too preoccupied with midwife school and clinicals, creating a book with my sisters, filming, and all of the typical household tasks. My schedule was busy.

The more Pops got to know Derick, the more he liked him and the more enthusiastic he became, especially because we both felt called to serve in full-time international missions. Pops began talking to me especially about Derick, even suggesting that we go see him sometime soon.

I hadn't given it much thought, but my initial reaction wasn't positive. "It just seems a little awkward," I replied. "I don't even know the guy!"

"Come on, Jill," he called. "That would be amazing. The network is discussing shooting us on a trip to Japan and China. When we're finished, we can easily see him in Nepal before flying home."

The trip made headlines, and it was undoubtedly a once-in-a-lifetime occasion. Even though we'd just returned from a vacation to Europe with the film crew two years prior, I was unaccustomed to such luxuries. I was still resolved not to lose my cool, so I kept it cool and told Pops I'd check to see if the vacation plans would coincide with my midwifery studies. It turned out they didn't, so the Japan and China trips went forward, but there was no chance of a Nepal swing.

Pops didn't push too hard, but he was patient and persistent, and another opportunity arose quickly.

In March 2013, we were on a road trip and staying with friends in Illinois when I stepped out of the house to get something from our bus. Pops was there alone, phone to his ear, smiling and conversing with someone. As soon as he saw me, he indicated for me to sit down and switched the call to speakerphone. It was Derick again, so I felt I knew how this was going to go: I would listen silently while Derick informed my father on his work, as he had done three or four times previously. This time, however, Pops did not keep my presence a secret.

"Hey, Derick," he said after a minute. "My daughter Jill is here with me. Why don't you introduce yourself and share your testimony with her?"

My face immediately turned red. I said, "You didn't tell me you were going to do that!" This is so embarrassing!, but Pops simply grinned and waved me off. I jabbed him in the ribs with my elbow. Pops' grin just widened.

"Hey, Jill," Derick said.

"Um, hey?" My voice shook like never before. "It's nice to meet you."

I felt glad when Derick took over the conversation. He told me a little about his upbringing—how he only had one brother, how his father died unexpectedly while he was a freshman at Oklahoma State, and how this pushed him to get out and accomplish something meaningful with his life. He talked about his time in Nepal and how much he enjoyed the mission field.

I said very little. Even if I had more questions, I didn't want to add to Pops' excitement. So I just listened, and after a few minutes, the talk ended. Derick appeared to be a kind person, but I wasn't interested in getting to know him. Instead, I dismissed the embarrassing phone call from my mind.

I was initially intrigued by the prospect of appearing on television while the show was still in its infancy. I wanted to see what it would be like, to see what would happen through the window of opportunity that God had provided for us. As the show progressed, my thoughts grew clearer. People would frequently ask me how I felt about everything, expecting that I liked it and that being on TV was the best thing ever. I always responded respectfully and tried not to make anyone feel uneasy, but their assumptions were incorrect.

While it was fun at times, and we had some fantastic adventures while filming the show, being on TV had its drawbacks. As each season was produced and televised, as more and more of the Duggar family's lives were broadcast to homes throughout the country, my opinion began to shift. The more I learned about what it meant to have your life become the focus of a reality TV show, the more I realised that, while it was still a ministry for Pops and the rest of us, it was something quite different for the network that created us. The show, and thus the entire Duggar family, was a money-making machine. No matter how much Pops talked about flying above New York City and the potential impact of reaching millions with Christ's message, we were there to entertain the company that paid the bills. We needed to keep things interesting, and we understood that if we didn't provide the audience stuff to connect with, there would be no show. If everything became stale, the game would be over.

Keeping things new necessitated careful planning and, on occasion, some rehearsal. Some of the finest TV moments were a guy asking Pops for permission to marry a Duggar girl, as well as the proposal itself, although there was little room for spontaneity. Every step would be practised in preparation. Bending the rules was occasionally necessary to keep things fresh. So, even if physical contact between courting couples was prohibited, we'd be permitted to wrap our arms around one another if the production needed it—which is exactly what happened in one episode featuring a bizarre triple date including an expensive archery competition.

What bothered me the most was how the show intruded on my most private moments. I was sixteen years old when I had my wisdom teeth extracted—my first surgical procedure. I dislike needles and was nervous about everything involved in the surgery, and knowing that it would be the main subject of an episode just made matters worse. But saying no to the cameras was not an option. Thinking about Mom was the one thing that brought me comfort. I knew she didn't want her birth filmed, but she went along with it nonetheless. If she can put up with it, so should I.

To keep things interesting, we had to dig deeper as the show progressed. Sometimes it was a matter of travelling abroad, such as the mission trip to El Salvador in seasons two and five, the epic adventure to China and Japan following season six, or other excursions to Israel, Britain, and Ireland. But we didn't have the budget or time to fill the show with just travel, so we had to explore closer to home for new and intriguing stuff. "There's no such thing as bad TV" was something the crew stated so frequently that it became our own family motto, repeated whenever we experienced a little problem, such as an unexpected trip to the emergency department. Big life events, particularly important milestones, were more enjoyable. Mom giving birth always boosted our ratings, but it wasn't the only life event that made for wonderful television. When our producer, Scott, learned that one of us was going to start dating, his eyes lit up like a Christmas tree.

Following the call on the bus, Derick and I began communicating on a daily basis, and the more we chatted, the more I loved him. So, ultimately, I found myself sitting on the recliner chair in Mom and Pops' bedroom, facing my father, while I called Scott and placed him on speaker so we could both hear. I was nervous, although knowing I had Mom and Pops' complete support. What I was about to say could not be reversed. What I was going to do could never be undone.

"Scott? "I have some news to share."

"Oh, really?"

"Yeah. I've got a dude.

"What? Nice! Who?" He seemed eager and genuinely glad for me, and for a moment I forgot we were in a business meeting.

"Yes, Scott." I have a dude. "And he is in Nepal."

"Yes!" he exclaimed, sounding even more enthusiastic than before. Then he kind of laughed and said, "I don't know anything about this story or this individual. But yes. Nepal has been on my bucket list since forever. "When are we going?"

We all laughed. "Yeah, I totally did this for you, Scott."

I had always liked Scott. He made filming enjoyable, and I trusted him too. But I'd been doing the program long enough to recognize the implications of what we were talking about.

"Scott, I have never met this guy before. We've only ever chatted over the phone or via Skype."

"Really? Oh. So that's even better. "This is an excellent story, Jill."

"I'm sure it is. But, I have a query. If we go over there and you film me meeting the guy for the first time, but it doesn't work out and we don't start dating, do you have to show it? I'm not sure how I'd feel about putting that out there, and I wouldn't want to put this person through it, either.

Scott's tone changed somewhat. "I get what you're saying, but if we're going to make the investment of flying you, your father, and a crew over there and spending all that time away from the regular production schedule, we'd have to air it regardless of how the relationship comes out. "I am sorry."

It was precisely the answer I had feared.

I didn't battle with the decision for long—Scott required an answer right away—but I did wrestle hard. I liked Derick and tried to explain what it meant to be part of my reality TV family. I despised the idea of things not working out and having it broadcast all over the world. I couldn't think of anything more embarrassing. However, this was my only opportunity to visit him in Nepal. If I didn't take it, would the opportunity for me and Derick ever come again? I also discussed the concept with Derick, as it included both of us.

Finally, the show won. I informed Scott that I was willing to attend. We discovered a couple of weeks in late November and began planning. For a while, everything seemed to be going well.

"Listen," he began over the phone as we were a month away from heading to Kathmandu. "We can't do it for two weeks during Thanksgiving. "It has to be five days."

"Excuse me?" I asked. "You can stay for five days if you want, but I need two weeks to decide if this guy is the person I want to spend the rest of my life with. I will do whatever you wish. We can film a pretend parting scene, and I'll cry for you, but I won't do it in five days. "I just can't."

That time, I won. The crew videotaped Pops and me during our two-day journey from northwest Arkansas to Nepal, as well as my and Derick's first meeting—a moment I wanted could have remained private. They then spent another five days shooting various activities in Kathmandu. Just before we faked our goodbyes for the program,

Derick asked me on camera if I wanted to start a formal relationship. My eyes were completely heartfelt.

Jill and Derick in Nepal after the film team left. We were grateful for the extra week together. We were able to get to know each other better, and there were brief moments during the days when Pops allowed us room and our feelings blossomed. For example, one evening, Pops was chaperoning us in the room he and I shared, but he eventually fell asleep. Derick and I sat on the end of the bed, eating hot chicken fried rice from homemade tinfoil dishes he had gotten from a street seller. We discussed everything and nothing, and when it was time to leave, Derick looked at me.

"Goodnight," he said. "I love you."

"Goodnight," I said. "I love you too."

I fell completely in love with Derick. He was polite and respectful, and Pops was clearly impressed with him. So when it was time to depart, I was very upset. I cried on his shoulder as I said my goodbyes in the car at the airport, and I grieved again on the long drive home.

The good news was that Derick's two-year missionary tenure was coming to an end, so he returned to Arkansas a few months later. (He was nice when his closest buddies had to wait downstairs at the airport so that the team could shoot my family greeting him alone first!) I was not shocked that the rest of the Duggar family quickly came to know and love him. He impressed my parents by rapidly finding a full-time job doing tax accounting at Walmart headquarters and enrolling in a seminary program, and everyone I met said he was friendly and sincere. Every time I heard those words, I felt myself sighing in relief. I'd discovered a guy I was in love with, who my parents approved of, and who wouldn't cause conflict in the family or interfere with filming. Derick was unique, and I couldn't let him go.

Derick returned to the United States in January 2014, but by the end of February, we were already talking about marrying. Derick proposed at the end of March, after successfully collaborating with Scott and the crew to deliver all of the elements of a terrific episode, and we began planning our June wedding.

On Easter Sunday, Derick called to tell me that his mother had been diagnosed with non-Hodgkin lymphoma.

"It's stage four," he explained. "The first doctor she saw refused to treat her and told her they couldn't do anything at this time. She found another doctor who gave her a second opinion, and he plans to begin intensive chemotherapy next week. But they haven't offered her much hope."

I was in Hot Springs, Arkansas, four hours away, chaperoning Jessa as she spent time with the guy she was courting. I felt the earth crumble all around me. Derrick's mother and I had been very close friends over the last few months, and she had told me how thrilled she was to finally be having a girl. I could not comprehend what Derick was going through, having previously lost his father and now being told that his mother was also likely to die. He would be left with only one sibling, and I couldn't imagine how that would have felt. When I tried to place myself in that situation, the feeling of loneliness was so dreadful that it was difficult to breathe.

But Derick was unlike me. As the days and weeks passed, I saw the strength of his character, the depth of his faith, and the power of the links of love that held his family together. He continued to work, checking in on his mother and assisting her as required, while supporting his lovely stepfather Ronnie, who cared for her around the clock. Derick continued to attend seminary, organise his wedding, and make himself available for filming. His desire and ability to work hard were impressive, and the more I learned about his mother, Cathy, the more it made sense. She faced her cancer diagnosis with fortitude and the kind of unwavering faith in God that takes a lifetime to develop. She refused to succumb to fear, telling everyone who asked how she felt that she was confident she would survive.

With Cathy's diagnosis, the wedding became much more personal. For a while, the fact that the day would be filmed and televised faded into the background. That did not last long. I was the first Duggar daughter to marry, and the network was anxious to make as much good television out of it as possible. As the big day approached, an increasing number of decisions were made with the show in mind.

Most of the time, I was fine with it. I didn't mind that the guest list had expanded to 2,000 people, or that some of them were utter strangers to me. I didn't care. I was focused on completing the wedding planning process and marrying my best friend. However, we encountered an issue with the photographs.

I wanted all of the guests to be able to take photos and then post them on an app with unique tags so that I could have copies of each one. The network didn't agree.

"They want exclusive rights," Pops explained, "and they are concerned that if we allow others to take images, they may leak. "They are offering to pay for photographers."

I was exhausted and stressed, so for a while I tried to dig in and stand firm—in the loveliest, most courteous way possible. However, my resistance did not last long. The pressure rose.

"This is not a hill to die on," Derick stated after the matter was brought up during a wedding planning meeting with my father and another network official. "We can let this one go." I reluctantly agreed with him.

The month leading up to the wedding was a haze, although I was aware that significant changes were taking place. There was talk that a new season of the show would be agreed upon. Also, Pops recruited someone to work with him for the first time, which struck me as unusual yet beneficial. My parents were becoming increasingly overwhelmed as the show's popularity grew. Pops had always kept things to himself, but there were times when I wondered if it was all becoming too much for him. So it made sense for them to seek assistance. Bringing in this new person, Chad, to assist with public relations, negotiations, and business agreements can only be beneficial.

Then there was the aeroplane. As our viewership increased, Mom and Pops spent more time going to various speaking engagements. It had gotten to be too much for them, so Pops purchased a four-seater, single-engine plane and arranged for a local pilot buddy to fly them when they needed to go. Being Pops, and knowing my brother John's childhood desire of becoming a pilot, he arranged for this guy to offer John aviation lessons, so John frequently joined them on flights to earn training hours. I was thrilled for my parents and John, and though I considered it momentarily, I didn't want to know how much the plane cost or where the money came from.

Then, eight days before the wedding, during our final planning meeting, Derick received a call.

Jill and Derick do interviews at the shop.

We were gathered at a nearby restaurant: Derek and I, Mom, Pops, and Jana, three of my wedding organiser pals. Derick and I had just returned from visiting his mother at the hospital, but before we could begin the meeting, his phone rang, and he stepped away from the table.

He didn't speak much during the conversation, only a few basic inquiries. I watched as blood drained from his face.

When it was over, he put his phone away, walked back, and looked at everyone. "I apologise." I think I have to leave. My mother has gotten worse. She is being airlifted by helicopter to a new hospital. She is not doing well. "It sounds serious."

At that point, everything changed. For weeks, my phone had been continually alerting me to a fresh message to respond to, a missed contact to answer, or an important choice that had been long overdue. I no longer had the ability to deal with it. If my sister Jana hadn't offered to take my phone and manage all of the wedding details for me in the last few days, I would have gone utterly insane.

In the days running up to the wedding, I spent as much time as possible at the hospital. Whenever we weren't there, I anticipated Derick to get another phone begging him to hurry back and be with his mother before she died. I was prepared for a hit, my insides constricted, and my heart was just about to break.

But the call never arrived.

The day before our wedding, we began to hope that Derick's mother might make it. She even mentioned joining us at church. "Mom says she'll be there," stated Derick. "I don't know how, but they're saying they will let her sign a release and let her out of the hospital on oxygen to be there."

It was the best news I'd ever heard, and I prayed she'd be able to make it. The day was a whirlwind, with the Big House packed and the noise, commotion, and laughing at an all-time high. After stopping by the hospital to check on Cathy, I rushed home to relocate some of my belongings before getting ready for the video wedding rehearsal run-through at the church that afternoon, followed by the rehearsal dinner that evening. My brothers were delighted to accompany Derick to his bachelor party after supper that evening, and my older sisters and I were giggling like preteens once more, since we were going to stay at a hotel for some additional sister time away from the craziness. Overall, it was a pleasant day, but one recollection jumps out more in retrospect than others.

"Hey," Pops said to some of the older siblings earlier that day. "Chad and I have been finalising details for the upcoming program, and I have some paperwork for you to sign here. "Can you do it quickly before you leave?"

"Sure," I replied, not thinking too much about it. Some of the big TLC and production folks who weren't typically in town were visiting, so I guess Pops was under more pressure than usual to get everything they needed together. "What's this for?"

"Oh, it's just about how you're gonna get paid."

I looked at the papers on the dining room table: single pages with signature lines and each of our names printed. Several had already been signed. I didn't see any extra papers to read, and I had no idea what it was about, so I didn't ask my father. After all, I'd never had a reason not to believe Pops. He knew best and always had.

So I picked up the pen and signed.

Chapter 4: Costs

Two hours before the wedding ceremony began—just after we'd completed an on-the-spot interview with People magazine—Derick and I were able to spend a few precious moments alone. We shared Chick-fil-A nuggets and attempted to keep the oil off our clothes. It was a lovely time, made even more special by a phone call Derick received regarding his mother. Cathy was coming to the wedding. She'd be in a wheelchair, on oxygen, and accompanied by a nurse who would make sure she stayed away from people to avoid contracting diseases, but she was coming. Waves of relief and gratitude washed over me.

The event made my already overflowing heart even more emotional. I wanted to be present, to experience every moment, every emotion. The beauty of the music we chose, the smiles on the faces of so many people I adored, the strength of the vows we exchanged, and the tenderness of my first kiss. Sometimes I just needed to halt and tell myself to breathe.

The rest of the day was normal wedding day mayhem, with the addition of a camera team, many official photographers, and uninvited paparazzi prowling outside, but I attempted to tune out the cacophony generated by the show.

Everything costs money in the realm of reality television. The shopping carts full of delicious food, the journey to Nepal to meet Derick in person for the first time, and the wedding itself all came at a cost, which we paid by allowing the cameras into our lives, giving them access to all the raw, unfiltered activity that would be offered up for entertainment. Don't get me wrong: it was a privilege to be able to benefit in that way. Being a Duggar on TV gave me opportunities and experiences that I would never have had otherwise. The performance gave me so much, and I am grateful for the locations I went, the experiences I had, and the people I met.

However, not all expenses are worthwhile. Some items aren't for sale.

Despite the emotional turmoil we were experiencing in the months leading up to the wedding, I was certain that our honeymoon would not be shown on the show. It was intimate and precious, and I was unwilling to trade it for an all-expenses-paid honeymoon. Josh and Anna's honeymoon to South Carolina was edited to make them appear inexperienced and naive, as if they had grown up in a sheltered environment and were about to have their first sex. The entire situation was embarrassing and intended to make them appear awful. I didn't want that for Derrick or me.

There was only a little pushback from the production team, but once we made it obvious that we would not be taking cameras on our honeymoon, they made it apparent that they would not be providing any financial assistance with the honeymoon. We took five days off and went to a beach in North Carolina. It suited us to keep things simple and short. Our bank balance was low, Derick only had a few days of vacation available, and with Cathy back home, still on edge from the wedding day, we were concerned about even going away at all.

We returned to see the astonishment and surprise on Pops' friends' faces as they worked on the house he was flipping—our first home as a married couple.

"What are you guys doing back so soon?"

"Aren't you supposed to be on your honeymoon?"

"We figured you'd be away the whole month."

I considered explaining Derick's work schedule and the fact that we were on a tight budget, but opted against it. Cathy was getting well, Derick and I had just started the application process to become missionaries, and I was just a few months away from finishing my midwifery examinations. My life as a married lady of twenty-three was finally starting. This was a time to look forward, not backward.

We returned from our honeymoon feeling as if we hadn't been gone at all. TLC wanted the wedding episodes to show as soon as possible, so Scott and his crew faced a tight timeline to film all of the interviews. Pops had recently converted one of the shops at the front of the Big House into a studio, so we only had to drive thirty minutes from where we lived in Rogers, but with Derick working forty-five hours a week as a manager at the Walmart home office with a team that handled the company's tax audits, we could only film in the evenings and weekends. I felt guilty for bringing him into it, but he had a positive attitude and rarely complained.

Days after the wedding, he received a call from his mother, Cathy, who was scheduled to have a scan that day to determine whether the first of six planned rounds of chemotherapy had had any effect. I had been praying ceaselessly. But as the phone rang and Derick put it on speaker, I couldn't help but feel panic rise in my gut.

"I've got news," she announced. "You know that chemo nearly killed me, don't you?"

Derick gave me an anxious look. "Yes, Mom."

"No, it didn't. But it appears that it killed the malignancy. The doctor says I am cancer-free. He said he didn't know how, but it must have been a miracle. She broke off laughing. "I told him that prayer works."

It was the finest news ever.

Then, on a Sunday evening, after only a month of marriage, I received more exciting news. I discovered I was pregnant.

I was exhausted and struggling with morning sickness, and Derick was attempting to focus on his work, but there was little time to unwind. We had filming to do almost every day after Derick completed work, and there was even more to do on weekends. Evenings were the hardest, and the crew would often become irritated with us if we were late or if Derick took longer than a few minutes to eat and change.

"Hey guys," Scott would call out from downstairs whenever they were filming at our place. "Come now. Time is running out. We do not want to be late again.

I understand why the crew was annoyed by having to wait for us, and they were probably unaware that we had never been paid for our filming and were working as volunteers. I'd never questioned it since that was how it had always been, from the beginning. And I'd been instructed not to discuss the show's inner workings or information with anyone for as long as I could remember. Furthermore, I would avoid implying or saying anything unfavourable about my parents. We were simply youngsters when the show first began, and all we knew was that it was Pops' show, and our job was to do anything he asked of us. requesting to be paid for appearing on the show seemed as insane to me back then as requesting to be paid for assisting in the construction of the Big House.

It was different now that Derick and I were married, and the twenty hours of filming we had to do each week soon became a strain for us. If we were lucky, we'd have it finished by nine p.m. Other times, we'd be filming till midnight. Ironically, this "family filming ministry," which emphasised putting your family first, was draining the life out of ours.

We both relished whatever minutes we had alone, where no camera crew could tell us to hurry up. I chose to drive Derick to and from work every day that I could, and our chats in the car became our safe haven, a place where we could open up about our day's concerns.

The show's topic was quickly brought up.

"All this filming," Derick commented as we drove away from the house at six thirty one in the morning. "It's hard."

We drove a little further in silence. Between the pregnant discomfort and the chills of worry produced by my old need for approval, I remained silent.

"And now that you're pregnant, it's much tougher. "Is it always like this?"

"I understand. It's difficult for me, too. Just a bit longer. When Jessa gets married and begins having children, maybe it will ease our weight and make things simpler for us."

Derick thought for a moment.

"You know what I wish?"

"No."

"That we could say 'this doesn't work for us,' and they'd make a change."

A new wave of nausea struck me. "Oh, darling, we cannot rock the boat. Not like that. "Not this soon after we married."

For a time, I wondered whether Derick would say something else. But he stopped, looked at me, and reached for my hand.

"I love you," he said, squeezing it in rhythm with each word.

"I love you too," I said. Four squeezes.

Mom and Pops, like all good IBLP parents, thought that their adult children—even those of us who had married and started our own families—were still under their parental authority. We were careful not to offend them, so we pretty much did whatever was expected of us, from dressing appropriately to agreeing to anything the program required. So, while we'd been able to hold our ground and keep our honeymoon private, it was impossible for us to control the announcement of my pregnancy. Josh and his wife Anna had three children by the time Derick and I married, and Mom had given birth six times since we began filming, so there was already a clear path that we had to take—not just in terms of some media outlet receiving exclusive rights to the official announcement, but also in terms of how we informed those closest to us. We were supposed to inform the producers first, and then, once they were ready to film it, we could notify our parents. I broke the rules a little by notifying a few of my sisters and friends beforehand, but when it came time to tell my parents and Derick's mother and stepfather, I made certain to follow the regulations.

I had to assure the team that if I informed them, we'd all keep it a secret, because we couldn't make a formal announcement for another month—due to the show still airing our wedding story and teasing my sister Jessa and Ben's blooming relationship and upcoming wedding. So, a few days later, with cameras rolling, we went over to the Big House and informed my folks. At first, it was exactly how I expected for any other family. The room was filled with enthusiasm and laughter, as well as some sibling taunting such as "You're gonna get so fat!" and "Derick's gonna love those diaper changes." It felt typical and enjoyable, and I found myself wanting to devour every moment of it.

A day or so later, the enchantment was broken.

I was swamped with emails, texts, and phone calls from the network and production crew as they worked to organise everything and ensure that "the announcement"—carefully planned so as not to detract from Jessa's wedding—went down without a hitch. Everyone expressed their excitement for us. I was tempted to remind everyone that it was my baby we were talking about, but I didn't want to be the crabby first-time mom. Not yet, at least.

TLC's talent management advised us that People magazine would own the story and would plan a photoshoot in the following days. We couldn't tell anyone but a small number of relatives and friends until People broke the story, and even then, we'd have to coordinate perfectly with them for our own child's birth announcement.

We were six years into the show and had been married for a little more than a month, and while I had never been pregnant before, I was familiar with the timing and restrictions, so not much of what they said surprised me. But as I explained the situation to Derick that evening, I could see the perplexity in his eyes.

"So we can't tell anyone else, and those we've told must swear to absolute secrecy," he replied, repeating what I'd just told him. "When the time comes to make an announcement, the magazine gets to post it first on their website. And then, two hours later, we may share on social media, just sharing our joy and encouraging others to read the complete story online or in print from others magazines, as well as reminding them to watch TLC for more. So basically, we get to make the announcement, correct?

"Right."

"And this is normal?"

"Yeah."

"But this is not natural. This is ridiculous, Jill! I don't enjoy being a dancing monkey who has to perform in these silly photo shoots. And I don't enjoy having to compromise on when and how we're going to post our own family announcements."

Derick's tone was controlled, but I could see he was frustrated about the limits. He started coming up with ideas, such as going rogue and posting our own pregnancy announcement. But as a good IBLP girl who followed her father's rules, I understood that was a no-no. I attempted to rein him in again.

"Babe, we cannot simply post our own family announcements. "TLC and my father would be furious."

"So we're essentially slaves to TLC and your dad. "Is that how it is?" Then Derick paused in frustration. "If it's this intense around the announcement, what's it going to be like with the birth?"

I knew the answer but did not want to tell him. Mom had learned how to manage the show's expectations for giving birth—allowing them access while being strict about which images they could capture. Josh's wife, Anna, had issues with the crew using film from one of her births, which she had explicitly told them she would not authorise. They edited it out for reruns, but with subsequent births, the film was frequently reinserted as part of flashback sequences.

I felt horrible for Anna and my mother for being forced to relinquish control over their labours. Their sole solace seemed to be that this was part of a God-given ministry. It was a significant expense to pay.

During my early pregnancy, I tried not to think about birth too much. I wanted to please everyone, but it seemed impossible. On the one hand, I wanted to make Derick happy and completely agreed with him that he did not want to give the network authority over the pregnancy and birth. However, according to IBLP teaching, Derick was also under my parents' authority and was expected to obey them.

Even though I was now Mrs. Jill Dillard, I remained Sweet Jilly Muffin. I wanted to impress everyone, including my husband, parents, and the network. I was in a state of turmoil and didn't know how to manage my emotions. All I knew for certain was that if I messed up and did not have my parents' blessing, I would be sinning by failing to obey God's plan.

Just when life was about to grow too intense, the clouds parted. Pops stated that he was taking a group of Duggars on a week-long mission trip back to El Salvador in December 2014, and he invited Derick and me to join them. Neither of us needed to ponder long before saying yes. Even though it would be a busy trip with less-than-ideal amenities, especially given that I would be nearing the end of my pregnancy, it sounded like a wonderful break from some of the turmoil and hard workdays at home. The irony of seeking comfort and relief from the difficulties of life in El Salvador, which had its own set of difficult stresses and conditions, was not lost on either of us.

Derick had spent two years in Nepal and had travelled extensively around Asia, but he had never visited Latin America before. I was eager to show him the project that my family had visited several times in the previous years, and I had a feeling he'd fall in love with the people, cuisine, landscape, and children there just as much as I did.

It lived up to all of my expectations.

Those five days provided a reprieve from everything that was making life at home stressful. My morning sickness had finally subsided, and for once, our schedule did not interfere with the rest of the Duggar family's. It was a comfort not to feel like we were disappointing others or making their lives miserable.

Better than all of that was the opportunity to see Derick in action. He didn't mind the heat or the lack of creature comforts, as long as he could help others and sit and converse with them about life, God, and everything else. I'd only seen a glimpse of this in Nepal, so it was a treat to see him come alive in El Salvador.

The journey was filled with memorable moments. Sleeping on an inflatable mattress on the church's front porch, portraying Mary and Joseph in the church's nativity play, and spending time together without the strain of filming. But the best part was witnessing Derick connect with the children at the orphanage. His mother was adopted, and it meant a lot to see the kids' cheeks light up as he and some of the other team members played soccer with them and had fun.

The day before we flew home, we were riding in the truck with Mike, the director of missions. He was explaining how they had begun working with ex-gang members, providing them with food, job training, and pastoral care, when he asked us a question I didn't expect.

"We could use a young couple like you down here, supporting the growing local church ministry and working with Indigenous leaders to provide jobs in gang communities, which would help people stay out of the gangs." Could you just pray about coming down and working with us? It would only be for a year, possibly two."

I was stunned. However, I was also curious. Derick and I shared eyes, and I knew he felt the same way.

A month later, after praying and seeking advice from individuals we trusted—including my parents and Derick's mother—we called Mike and told him we were in, pending certain details. We explained that we wanted to wait a few more months before moving so that I could give birth in April and ensure everything went well for both me and the baby. Mike was pleased, and Derick and I were excited. Those morning and nightly vehicle chats on the way to and from his work were no longer about the stress of filmmaking, but about this new adventure that our little family was about to embark on.

The closer we went to April and my due date, the more I considered what the show may expect from the birth. Mom and Anna had let the cameras in for all of their births, but I wasn't so sure. My midwifery training had taught me what could go wrong, and I knew enough about myself to know that at that most intimate, vulnerable area of labour, I'd value my privacy more than ever. But keeping the cameras out didn't seem feasible.

When I originally brought this up with Derick, he saw no problem. "We can just tell them what we want to do," the man replied.

"Babe, no." You do not comprehend. That is not how it is. We can't just tell them what we do and don't want."

Derick frowned. "However, this is not like an engagement or birth announcement. "This is birth..." He left it hanging.

"Yeah," I replied. "But… they have certain expectations."

We returned to the subject several times, but it always seemed like we were trapped in the same place. Derick couldn't comprehend how the show could wield so much power over the birth, and after more than a decade in front of the cameras, I couldn't see how we could ever hope to fight for what we wanted. We were locked in a loop, and the birth was approaching.

Finally, Scott brought it up one evening after we had completed filming. It was just him and us in the house—no Pops, no Chad—which seemed like the greatest way to begin.

"So," he said, like a chef describing a dinner he was preparing. "This is how we are thinking about the birth. TLC wants to do it well, so we're talking about a couple of one-hour specials. One will be a quick turnaround show that will air within a week of the birth, assuming all goes as planned. For that one, we'll have all of the lead-up footage previously shot, with a spot reserved at the end for a few minutes of the delivery before it airs. Then there's the other special, which will be a more detailed account of the birth in a follow-up program that will most likely run three weeks later. "How does that sound, guys?"

I took long breaths to calm myself, as I had seen many moms, doulas, and midwives do. "I don't feel comfortable taping the birth, Scott. As a student midwife, I already feel anxious about the birth because I know too much, and I know I'll be preoccupied with my thoughts. Furthermore, I do not want to feel like a watched pot.

Scott sat back. "Okay," he said, struggling with the puzzle. "How about we do what we did with Anna's last two? I'll just be outside with a camera, and I'll come in and take a few shots whenever you want."

Take another breath. This time, it's even deeper. "No. I don't even want it, Scott. "I do not want it filmed."

Scott burst into tears. He'd been on the show virtually from the beginning, and we'd been through a lot together. He'd been everywhere we'd gone and had experienced all of our important occasions. He was Uncle Scott, and I felt bad talking to him like that. However, there was a small part of me that wondered whether he was crying because of the pressure TLC was placing on him to agree to record the birth.

"It is not you, Scott." You're great. It's me. If I'm stressed, I won't be able to get this baby out."

"Okay," he replied, sitting up straight. The mood had shifted. I knew the dance. Whatever happened next would be his last offer. "What if we gave you some cameras?" Your mom and Jana will be there, correct?"

I nodded. This was his final offer, the concession I had to make. If I had refused to shoot home video with my mother and sister, I would have faced an even more difficult battle. Pops and the entire network would undoubtedly get involved. I wasn't sure whether Derick and I could survive such a force.

My aspirations for a natural birth were dashed on the third day of labour. When my water broke, I tried to start labour at home with the midwife. It would start and stop repeatedly. After more than forty hours of this, we decided to visit the hospital. Another twenty-four hours passed, first with Pitocin and then with an epidural, but no baby. In fact, following the epidural, the baby found himself in an undeliverable position known as breech transverse—just him chilling in a hammock-like position. I was fatigued. So, after sixty-eight hours of labour, Israel David Dillard was born via C-section on April 6, 2015. Between all the drugs I was on and the gowns, screens, and bright lights required for the surgical procedure, Scott ended up getting a lot more footage from my mom and Jana's cameras than he'd probably expected—a lot more than if the labour had occurred naturally and simply in a birth pool in my bedroom. But he did not receive everything. Derick had his own video camera with him, and we had agreed that everything he caught would be just for us.

As I sat in my hospital bed, staring in awe at this lovely baby boy as he nursed, I realised my mind was clouded by post-partum hormones. I felt like an astronaut who had just returned to earth, confused about what had happened. But I was able to think clearly enough to be concerned that Derick would fail to follow the birth plan that Chad and the network had put out for us—People magazine would reveal first, and as a family, we would only use photographs they approved. If any images or news were released, we'd be in danger.

Between the dread of not satisfying all of the network's requirements, keeping the news from spreading too quickly, and the guilt over our personal private videoing of the birth, I felt like I was rebelling against Pops, which I wasn't sure how I felt about. Even though all of the conversations about the show's access to my labour had taken place between me, Scott, and Derick, I knew that almost everything we'd discussed would have been shared with Pops, especially if it caused an issue. The show remained his show, and even as his children grew up, married, and had their own children, we continued to provide many of the wonderful TV moments that kept the ratings high. More than that, even though I was married and a mother of my own, I was still my father's daughter. When he stated he'd give me to Derick at the wedding altar, it was a meaningless gesture. The IBLP doctrine made it apparent that his influence over me would never be diminished. If I defied him or did not fulfil his requests and left the safety of the umbrella, I would put myself in danger.

I was naive to it at the time, but I would ultimately realise how damaging and toxic the IBLP's authority doctrines were in my life. The umbrella principle sounded innocent enough when I was a child, but it was a brutally efficient way of creating fear and controlling conduct in the lives of others, whether they were adults or children. The worry of what would happen if I walked out from under this umbrella had permeated every aspect of my life, leaving me questioning so many decisions. Even hiding a camera from Scott in the hopes of preserving my modesty and keeping the rest of the world from seeing me give birth felt risky. My father wanted us to assist with the show, so fooling Scott may be interpreted as sinful rebellion against him if he opposed. I could be outside the umbrella, and something awful could happen.

I was worried about Derick, afraid he'd do or say anything that would hurt Scott, but he stuck to the plan. For the sake of our marriage, he stepped under the umbrella with me, despite later telling me how strange and angry he felt when the first photo he ever saw of Israel was when Pops stepped out of my hospital room and showed him the photo he was going to send to Chad for People magazine.

We settled into our new lives, enjoying our new baby as much as we could in between filming as we prepared to leave for El Salvador. Summer was just a few weeks away, our first anniversary was quickly coming, and we were learning to flow with the rhythms of a newborn infant. Even the shame of hiding things from Scott and Pops began to disappear.

And then, one evening in May 2015, Derick and I were in the Big House when Pops entered the room, looking exhausted and concerned. He appeared to have forgotten how to maintain the smile that he wore so often.

He gathered several of the elder ones about him and talked gently, choosing his words as if he were navigating a minefield.

"I just heard that a tabloid published information on events that occurred a long time ago. Things that transpired between Josh and the girls."

I was shocked. Nobody spoke. We just waited for Pops to continue.

"In Touch magazine has obtained a copy of the police report from the investigation. I'm not sure how they obtained it, but I'm told the material it includes is graphic."

Nobody breathed.

Silence.

"I'm doing everything I can to make them stop. I am certain that what they are doing is illegal, and I want to stop it."

The remainder of the evening was a blur. My brain was spinning. All I wanted was to get home, close the doors and windows, and forget about everything that had happened. I wanted to dive so deep that none of these memories would ever surface again. And if that didn't work, I hoped Pops could somehow shut this down.

The one constant source of peace I could find was observing Israel as he ate and slept. I didn't believe I could love him any more than I did the day he was born, yet when the world around me threatened to explode, watching my precious boy kept my heart steady.

When daylight arrived, there was no point in hiding. Derick needed to go to work, and I had a doctor's appointment. Because I hadn't entirely healed from my C-section, I couldn't hoist Israel in his car seat, so Jessa came over to drive me to the appointment. I was grateful for that. It felt like a day to be by your sister's side.

On the way to the appointment, I attempted to distract myself by staying in the now and thinking about what else I needed to do that day. I told myself everything was OK, but there was a knot in my stomach, a string wrapped tightly around my throat. At times, it felt like the air was running out.

We had barely parked, and Jessa was about to grab Israel out of the back seat when Pops called.

"They released it. "I am sorry."

Jessa and I immediately burst into tears.

"They promised us secrecy," I continued, finally able to speak. "They claimed it was private. That it was a safe environment. "How could this happen?"

I was in shock all afternoon. I couldn't believe that what I had told individuals in confidence at the Child Safety Center all those years ago had been made public. I could readily recall how much it had cost me to talk about what had happened with Josh—how terrible it had been to relive those memories, and how terrified I was that we would be separated from my parents as a result. How could anyone participating in that process be willing to share it with the media?

The sense of shock did not endure very long. Worse was on the way, like an avalanche rumbling down a valley after a stormy night. For when I eventually mustered the nerve to visit the In Touch website and read the story for myself, I was immediately overcome with a deep, all-encompassing, overpowering sense of fear.

They'd published everything. All of the investigation's details, which we had previously revealed in hushed whispers with teary eyes, were suddenly emblazoned across the screen. However, it was not presented solely in the cold, forensic language of the initial report. This was tabloid journalism at its worst. The most vivid, scandalous, and distressing elements of the narrative had attracted the most attention. It was written just for the sake of enjoyment.

As soon as I heard Derick's key in the lock that evening, I ran to him. He hugged me tightly and grieved beside me. I told him about the abuse when we were almost engaged, a little over a year ago. The report's release stung him even more, and he was furious. It required all of his self-control to be cool for me.

"Hey. "How are you doing?"

"Terrible," I replied. I'm an avoidant by nature, but there was no getting around this. The weight was sufficient to crush me. "I wish I were dead."

That is all there was to say. I could not say much more. I just cried.

The nightmares began that night. It had been more than a decade since the initial torture, and I had never imagined what had happened. However, as soon as In Touch published the tale, the trauma began to manifest itself in my dreams.

Daylight did not provide much relief.

The doorbell rang shortly after Derick left for work, and I didn't think twice about who it was or what they wanted. I looked out as I typically would, and saw an unexpected package on the ground as well as someone walking right past the network's security guard who had let him pass. I halted, watching the delivery man return to his car, pick out a camera with a long lens, and point it at the front door. I peered closely. There were more of them.

They were there all day. All I could do to defend myself was keep the blinds down and avoid the yard, which was clearly visible from the road. I was imprisoned. I wanted to hide underneath a rock. I had spent my entire childhood being taught the importance of modesty and that it was my obligation as a godly woman not to behave or dress in such a way that any guy would have impure thoughts. And now the entire world might read and picture what had happened to me. I felt naked, ashamed, and degraded. I was being paraded around the streets, and my sexual abuse was being used as entertainment.

I spent a long time on the phone that morning. I spoke with my sisters, dad, Cathy, and Derick when he had a break. They were all loving and supportive, and I appreciated them all. We were all struggling together.

Talking with people I trusted did not alleviate my feelings of humiliation and shame, but it did help to clarify who I held responsible for everything: the chief of police at the time, Kathy O'Kelley; the city of Springdale and its attorney, Ernest Cate; and the Washington County Sheriff's Office and its major sheriff, Rick Hoyt.

The magazine, In Touch, its parent firm Bauer, and any other undisclosed players.

In the months and years since, many people have expressed their thoughts on how I handled the report's release. Some people offered their support and understanding, and I am grateful to them. However, others have accused me of blaming the wrong individuals. They claimed I was covering for my parents and that it was Mom and Pops' fault that everything happened in the first place.

It wasn't, and I am not.

I hold Josh accountable for his behaviour.

And I hold In Touch, Bauer, Kathy O'Kelley, Ernest Cate, the city of Springdale, the Washington County Sheriff's Office, and Rick Hoyt accountable for illegally releasing and publishing the report—for subjecting me and my sisters to the trauma of a second victimisation, which was made even worse by the fact that it was so public.

I am aware of the mistakes my parents, particularly Pops, have made in our upbringing over the years, but the way my parents handled or did not handle things with Josh has no bearing on or justifies the release of juvenile records and the further re-traumatization and exploitation of vulnerable victims.

The paparazzi were everywhere. When we left the house, they would follow us in their cars, their lenses trained on us like snipers. They attempted to contact Derick at work, and there were a large number of people camped out at the Big House. A friend of Pops' invited everyone to stay at his ranch in Oklahoma, so my family decamped there in the hopes of finding tranquillity.

Derick and I paid a visit over the weekend. I could feel myself exhaling as soon as we pulled off the road and entered the property. It was serene out there at the ranch, strange to be in a location of such tranquillity while everything else in our world was dominated by trauma. However, even though the ranch was free of photographers, it could not relieve our family's stress. The suspense was palpable the moment we went into the cabin that had become Duggar HQ.

The family was distributed over the room. Some were playing board games, while others were preparing to go for a walk. Mom was with the youngest children, while Pops was in the corner with Chad, his right-hand guy.

Josh and his family were also present. This may appear unusual, but I believe events were considered as a "thing of the past" by that time. It had been roughly three months since I'd seen Josh. He travelled to Washington, DC, in 2013 to work for a conservative organisation that opposed access to stem-cell research, abortion, divorce, and pornography (ironically, given later events). As soon as the story emerged, he resigned, and he, Anna, and the children fled the paparazzi and returned to Arkansas.

I didn't know how to be around Josh. Although what had happened had been handled and he had apologised numerous times, we no longer discussed it. It seemed like the distant past. Even so, I didn't expect him to be so easygoing. Later on, when he recalled being under siege by cameras, I didn't expect him to start laughing—even if it was plainly uneasy laughter.

It was strange that he was acting this way, but it was Mom who handled it.

"Josh," she demanded. "It's not your responsibility that this was revealed, but you should be aware that you were behind it all. "Do not be so arrogant."

Josh's smile disappeared. "I'm sorry," he replied. "I'm sorry to you, girls, that y'all are having to go through all this."

Pops was in game planning mode. He and Chad spent the most of the day huddling together, debating the best next steps and frequently accepting calls. They'd give snippets of news, but it wasn't until the evening that we could all sit down and listen to Pops explain everything to us.

He began by stating that TLC had suspended the show and was considering cancelling it completely. It seemed terrible for him to say it aloud, so he let the words linger in the air for a long time. It was difficult to see Pops like. It's difficult to watch him wounded. I couldn't imagine what life would be like for him, Mom, and my younger siblings without the show. But the fight was not completely gone from him.

"Some people want us to fade away. The world would like us to close our doors and disappear. But we aren't going to do that. We will not give up on this ministry. The window of opportunity that God has provided for this family to demonstrate to the world what it means to follow him remains open. They say we're damaged goods, but I'll work with TLC to see what we can do to get this thing up and running again."

Another pause. Then there was resolve in his voice again. Pops was Pops again, gathering his forces.

"It was wrong what Josh did," he continued, gazing at us all. "But we'll get through this. We'll move on. We need to make TLC understand that this happened in the past and is something we've previously dealt with."

In many ways, he was correct. This belonged in the past, and we had taken action to address it. During the DHS investigation, I met with a professional counsellor as recommended by the court, and my parents were always willing to listen if I wanted to chat. But by the end of the investigation, I didn't want to talk about it, so it was rarely brought up. Maybe it would have been useful for me to have had some early counselling when it originally happened, and it would have certainly been helpful around the time all of this was released in 2015, but, like many others, I didn't realise I needed it. So I buried it in the past.

The longer they chatted, the worse I felt. I felt sorry for my parents. Unfortunately, they had to do all of this. Unfortunately, Pops' show was on the line here. Unfortunately, the world was unable to recognize that my parents were nice people simply trying to do good.

So, even before they asked us females how we felt about them having a television interview, I knew what I was going to answer. I knew they needed someone to advocate for them, someone to vouch for them. They needed someone to do everything they could to preserve the show.

I was one of the older kids, so I had a greater sense of responsibility to do something, to help in some way. And I wanted to support them, to show them my love and commitment during this difficult moment. But I had no boundaries or understanding of what I needed to do to defend myself. I was afraid and didn't want to do the interview at all, but I knew it was the only way to demonstrate my love and dedication to my parents. I could clear their name and assure everyone that my brother's difficulties were resolved. How could I remain silent?

I assumed I understood how much it would cost me.

All of the trauma I had been experiencing while hiding behind closed blinds at home was about to worsen. That embarrassment, humiliation, and sentiments of being abused and violated all over again were about to be amplified. Everything was about to grow worse, but this was the price I had to pay.

"I would be willing," I responded. "I'll do the interview."

A rush of nausea hit me like nothing I had ever felt before. The room was whirling, with the sound of blood pouring into my ear. I understood why I did it, but what had I done?

Then, unexpectedly, a moment of hope.

"Me too," replied Jessa. "I'll do it with you."

Pops glanced at both of us. "Are you sure?"

We nodded.

"Thank you," he responded. "Thank you."

"Thank you," another voice replied. I looked up. It was Josh.

The subsequent days were hectic. Chad wanted to go over the talking points with us, and Jessa and I discussed how we could vouch for Mom and Pops. In an odd sense, I was relieved that there was no time to pause, to consider what was coming or how I'd feel about appearing on primetime TV to discuss the abuse. I was about to face the firing squad, and all I wanted to do was get this over with.

Chapter 5: Tearing Apart

"Do you still want to go?"

In the immediate aftermath of the release, Derick and I had not discussed going to El Salvador. But it was getting near. Decisions needed to be made.

It had been less than two weeks since Jessa and I met with Megyn Kelly. On that day, we sat beneath the dazzling lights of the Big House and did everything we could to support our parents. Answering all of Megyn's questions while Josh watched from a couch just out of shot was like removing a bandage from a deep and open sore. It was anguish, so excruciating that I didn't even think to question why Josh was allowed to be there in the first place. Worse, I had hoped it might alleviate the situation. It had not. The photographers were still hunting us, and the internet was still eating at us, reading over every network statement, new photo, and new viewpoint. My nightmares were growing worse, and there was nothing I could do to block them out. All I was doing was surviving one breath at a time.

So yes, I wanted to go. I felt it was something we were meant to do. But I was aware of the risks. As missionaries for this organisation, we would be responsible for raising our own financial support. The event provided us with far more exposure than we could have achieved on our own, but it also introduced certain challenges. We were aware that we could be considered as a target, so we elected not to announce our destination and just discussed working in Central America. We didn't want anyone to be able to track us down.

The first thing that occurred? Someone tracked us down. At least, that's what Derick and I assumed when we landed in El Salvador and Mike informed us that he had just received a call from a Salvadorian journalist who wanted to come and write about the mission.

Something about it did not add up. The mission was small, and other than from Derick and my arrival that month, nothing else had changed—certainly nothing that would pique a journalist's attention and compel them to visit.

Mike did not share our suspicions. He told us that he knew the journalist in question and had been questioned by him before. Nonetheless, I was relieved when the baby and other obligations kept me away from that area of the mission, out of the journalist's view, on the day he arrived.

Mike apologised a few days later, as the Sun published a grainy photo of Derick at the mission, along with a narrative about how we escaped Arkansas and were apprehended in El Salvador. He was kind, but it was too late. The poem had not only named the country we were in, but also named the mission itself. The target on our back had just gotten much bigger and brighter.

To make matters worse, we quickly discovered that there had been a significant surge in gang violence in the neighbourhood. There were suspicions of murder and kidnapping, as well as whispers that the wealthy were a particular target.

Despite the constant worry of being caught up in gang violence, life in El Salvador had some positive aspects. We stayed on the mission's grounds while a mission multipurpose house was being built overlooking a valley densely populated with banana trees and other jungle flora I didn't know. My days were divided between caring for Israel and leading groups of local women and girls. We had no air conditioning, no Wi-Fi, inconsistent power, and a swarm of fire ants trying to take over the kitchen. It took some time to adjust, but growing up in a large family taught me to be patient and accept that I might not always have everything I desired. We had been living comfortably for years thanks to the show, but I didn't miss the comforts. It felt fantastic to learn how to do laundry without all of the normal appliances, as well as how to clean food while being mindful of tainted water.

Arkansas and being part of a filming family felt a little further away, and I was grateful for the extra space. The show continued to capture our attention, and we spent a lot of time on our own with emails, talks, and filming. However, the location and pace of life made it simpler to deal with the filming requirements that remained with us, necessitating the occasional travel home. We took advantage of the moments of peace that this basic life provided whenever possible.

I was also happy for the opportunity to see Derick in mission mode again. He thrived on the job, and I was certain that I had never seen him so calm or comfortable as when he was seated on the back balcony, looking out over the valley, his Bible open on his lap and his notebook ready beside him.

"Hi, darling. "I just read something about Josh," he explained. "People say he was caught logging in to a website called Ashley Madison, which is for people who want to have extramarital affairs." I looked it up on Google, and there are several tabloids that are covering the topic."

My heart sank in my chest.

But I am determined to do things differently this time, to be active rather than passively waiting for the drama to unfold. I needed to know the truth, so instead of ignoring it, waiting for my parents to tell me what was going on, or attempting to gain information from my siblings, Derick and I felt it would be best if I texted Josh immediately. I wanted to hear straight from him, to see if the stories were true.

A day or two later, Mom called. "It's been devastating for Anna and the kids," she replied, her voice weary and irritated, just as it had been in the Oklahoma cabin a few months before. She confirmed the accusations, stating that Josh had admitted to being hooked to pornography for years and had paid to join a social networking site for those looking to cheat on their marriages.

By the end of the call, I was just as tired and angry with Josh and the situation as Mom.

This time, it was up to me to inform Derick.

"What happens now?" he inquired.

"He is being sent away," I groaned. "Again."

We had promised to work with Mike's mission in El Salvador for two years, but we had certain prior commitments back in the United States, primarily related to my midwifery studies, that required us to return home shortly. So, shortly after Josh's affair became public, we flew back to Arkansas and returned to Tontitown.

It was fall, a season full of wonderful memories of home—trips to Silver Dollar City, our favourite theme park, and extended games of Bible charades at home, in which one older sibling would lead three or more younger siblings in re-enacting anything from David and Goliath to Stephen's stoning. We had a great time back then, but when we returned from El Salvador, the Big House seemed different to me. There was no Scott, no TV cameras, and no visitors waiting in Pops' office; the Big House had lost its customary energy. It was sombre. Mom seemed exhausted. A number of my siblings appeared stressed. But that evening, when we gathered with the rest of the Duggar family in the living room for Bible time, Pops had some news to impart.

"Hey guys," he began after we had exchanged greetings and hugged, and everyone had made a fuss over Israel. "I just spoke with Josh and the guy who runs the hotel where he is living. He seemed to be doing well. He has been working in the kitchen. And the program's director believes he's doing great. He stated that he has served as a role model for some of the others and is their best person there.

Mom had told me about the Christian-run recovery clinic in Rockford, Illinois. I had little idea about rehab, but it seemed better than sending him away to work construction.

"We had some trouble getting him up there," remarked his father. "The paparazzi were trying hard to figure out where he was headed. They even followed the tail number of his aircraft. But at least we got him in there without being seen. According to the program's director, some photographers arrived at the open chapel in search of Josh. But the staff has been really nice to us, and they were able to keep him out of sight. I just wanted to let everyone know that we are pleased with the report and pray that God will continue to work in his life while he is there.

The conversation quickly changed, but his comments remained in my head like a bell. Though I loved my parents and understood why they would want to protect and care for their child, I couldn't help but wonder how far Pops had gone to safeguard Josh's privacy and keep him from being publicly humiliated. I discussed this to Derick, who confirmed that he had experienced the same thing. The feelings intensified within me, and by the time I went to bed, I felt sick to my stomach.

When the In Touch story broke, all I wanted was to be safe. All I needed was privacy and space to grieve without feeling the need to solve the situation. I knew that in the end, we'd all do everything we could to fight for justice in the legal system that had failed us, including filing a lawsuit against the magazine and those responsible for the illegal distribution of the documents. I also knew my father would fight hard, and I was quite grateful for his support. But as we were there in that cabin talking about the show, all I wanted was for Pops to say, "No, we're not going to put you on Fox News." I will do everything I can to keep you girls out of this. "We are no longer concerned about the future of our show." I wanted my father to stick up for me in that way. Did he know that? Would he have done things differently if I had spoken up? I had no idea. I'd spent most of my youth listening to IBLP lectures on the "umbrella of protection." When I needed it the most, it failed me. It felt like as a woman, I was expected to do everything I could to protect Pops and Josh. Nobody appeared to view things differently.

We were back in the US for a few weeks, and we spent a lot of time at the Big House. It was nice to be with the family, especially because there were no TV crews for a few weeks until everything resumed normally. Though our show and all of the reruns were pulled from regular airtime when everything was leaked in May 2015, filming didn't stop for long. My mother, Jessa, and I had already shot one scene for the network in August in New York City, and there was talk of additional program ideas resuming shortly. In between preparing for my forthcoming exam, we were quite busy catching up on doctor visits while also continuing to raise support and meet with individuals to update them on our mission. For a while, it seemed like a normal family.

Unlike TV networks, real families do not have meetings to pitch new shows. That is what happened one day in mid-September, when we returned home. Pops introduced the network men, and I recognized the gal who spoke first. I'd seen her at several media appearances, most recently during the Megyn Kelly interview. She might have even attended my wedding. I was unsure. With a guest list of 2,000, it was hard to keep track of who had and hadn't attended.

"We don't want to punish the victims," she explained, glancing around. "We've been trying to find out how to get the show back up and running. We'll start by focusing on the older kids who are adults, particularly those who are married and have moved out of the family. We may eventually be able to show the younger kids and your parents, but Josh will not be on the show. We cannot have him involved at all.

I could feel the entire audience moving its attention to Josh's wife, Anna. She remained still and quiet, like a rabbit expecting a hunter would simply move on.

"Before we continue," said the network official, "we want to make sure that you guys are on board."

Our producer, Scott, spoke up. "We'll have to rebrand the show with a new name and a completely new filming style—no more cutting back to old videos like previously. "Everything is new and fresh." He halted and looked at the older children. "We can't bring the show back without you. "What do you say?"

Despite what I had just heard, it felt like a watered-down version of the Oklahoma cabin chat to me. I wanted to aid Pops and show him that I was on his side, but at what cost? I wasn't sure if Derick or I saw much place for the show in our futures. The mission field was where our hearts belonged.

My siblings were taking turns expressing their support and agreeing to the new show. When it was time for Derick and me to talk, he mentioned how complicated our lives had become now that we were in El Salvador. "It's dangerous down there," he explained. "If we draw too much attention to ourselves or the mission, it could cause problems." We wanted to help, but we made it clear that our role would likely change immediately. We'd be gone again shortly, and when we returned to Central America, as promised, we wouldn't be returning to the United States for several months. If they were going to have us on the show, they'd have to be adaptable and imaginative, especially because they were considering calling it Jill and Jessa: Counting On. We wanted them to know that Derick and I were 100% committed to pursuing our missionary calling. The representative listened and then mentioned that we have consent over all content. Derick and I shared eyes, and I knew he, like me, believed it might work.

After we had all agreed, the representative had one last point to make.

"If we're going to perform the program again, we can't simply ignore what happened. Anna will have to sit down and talk about the affair, while the rest of you will have to discuss what happened with the magazine. "Will you be okay with that?"

We all froze. I don't think any of us were pleased with that, but the play had already begun with the Megyn Kelly interview. Going on TV, disclosing our most excruciating wounds for the sake of ratings, was what it looked like to be a TV family.

I felt for Anna. She had been through so much previously. And now things were going to grow worse.

Even though we had committed to return to the United States before starting our mission in El Salvador, spending six weeks there so soon after starting our work at the mission was not ideal. When we returned to El Salvador in December, Mike requested that we commit to staying until the following July. No more return trips to the United States. We happily agreed. We wanted to be 100% committed at all times.

When we returned, things felt different. It wasn't simply the twenty-two hundred miles between us and Arkansas, or the difficulty with communication. The new program represented a new beginning, and we had made significant adjustments to how we dealt with people in charge. Earlier this year, around the time we were departing for Central America, we established a 501c3 and requested Chad to assist us with fundraising. When we returned in the fall and filming resumed, we decided to ask him to be the network's primary point of contact. Suddenly, it didn't feel like Pops was asking us when we could film or what we could commit to, and we hoped that would help the program become more balanced and feel less burdensome. With Chad on our side, we hoped to sidestep some of the passion that came with negotiating our participation in the event. For a while, I felt optimistic. Perhaps the commitment would be manageable, and the program would provide Derick and I with just enough visibility to continue gathering the finances we needed to stay on the mission field.

There was another reason things felt different. El Salvador's gang situation has deteriorated during our absence. There were many more police officers on patrol in the capital, San Salvador, and some of the shops and houses in our small community had begun to hire armed guards. We'd had our own guard since we came, but it didn't seem like much safety anymore.

One evening, while Derick was out, I was inside our church room with a couple of the team's females. We lived in a quiet, rural area, so we all heard the single gunshot that resonated across the valley. We froze. It was close. We panicked when the second gunfire rang out shortly after. Two of the older women rushed me into a closet, and as I crouched on the floor with Israel close by, I heard the sounds of feet rushing around while the others looked for places to hide.

Minutes passed. It was hot inside the closet. The air was stale and lifeless. I listened intently, but there was no sound from the other side of the closet doors. I didn't know if that was a good sign or not.

My pulse was racing in my chest, and the sound of blood in my ears was almost deafening. I wanted to shout out and see what was going on, but if this was a probable kidnapping, our safety hinged on remaining hidden.

Israel began to wriggle, letting me know that he was as hot. He took a deep breath and made the sounds he typically makes just before crying. I fed him, frantically hoping that it would help.

After about ten minutes, someone gave the all clear. One of the guards at the other end of the property had been showing off by allowing a friend to shoot his gun.

At first, I felt relieved. Then I was irritated that the entire situation had been caused by someone acting so carelessly. As the sky darkened, I became concerned. My dreams that night were not set in a gloomy Arkansas bedroom.

Gunfire was rarely heard, and life began to settle into a rhythm. Each week presented a plethora of opportunities to pray with others, for Derick to preach, for us to visit a local orphanage, and to generally spend quality time as a mother of a young child with other mothers and their newborns. My family had been visiting the mission for years, and I was relieved that many of the folks we worked with considered us friends. In the weirdest of ways, I felt at ease down there.

As Christmas neared, it was time for the yearly mission trip to El Salvador. As usual, a few Duggars arrived, including Pops and several of my siblings—as well as a new acquaintance of theirs, a wonderful man named Jeremy, whom my sister, Jinger, was getting to know.

Six months had passed since we established Dillard Family Ministries, our 501c3. We had blogged about it on our family blog, and many people had responded generously. The early outpouring of financial support was incredible, but since moving, fundraising has become much more difficult. Money was going out of our ministry bank account faster than it was entering. Like any other missionary family, we quickly realised that fundraising while on the field is difficult. Things were a little more tricky for us because we were on TV—and we'd had a few comments on Twitter from folks who assumed we were making a lot of money from the show and shouldn't be asking for help. Derick wanted to set the record straight, stating that we made no money from the performance and that our participation was entirely voluntary, but he remained silent at my request. We believed that if we could do a good job of presenting what we were doing, and Chad could assist us with sending updates and even organising church events and meet-and-greets when we returned to the United States, fundraising would become a bit simpler.

The mission house that Mike's ministry had been working on was finished in time for us to move in during the first week of December, just before the Christmas mission team arrived. Mike was thrilled to show us around, and a few days later, when Pops and some of my siblings arrived with the rest of the team, we showed them around as well. The house was very empty, so Mike brought Pops and a few other people to the city one day to shop for some necessities. They returned with a washing machine, a rice cooker, and a few further items. That was a good day for a mom with a baby in reusable diapers.

A few nights during the trip, Pops, Derick, and I sat in our dimly lit bedroom, nursing Israel to sleep. It was a typical night on the outskirts of the jungle, and we were all exhausted by the 90-degree heat and 100 percent humidity. Our single fan was ineffective under these conditions.

I'm not sure who brought it up, but we somehow began talking about the show, the production schedule, and our availability. Suddenly, without notice, the conversation went to a topic I had always avoided discussing with my parents. Money.

Derick, with his accounting experience, had always paid close attention to our money, and he was beginning to worry that the initial fundraising might not be sustainable in the long run. As we continued to discuss ministry fundraising efforts and keeping supporters informed via frequent ministry email and blog updates, we were also reminded of our own personal finances.

Even though our ministry finances were completely independent from our personal finances, they influenced our thinking. Since the premiere of the new, rebranded show—Jill and Jessa: Counting On—we couldn't help but wonder when we may see some money for all of our prior and current efforts.

After returning to El Salvador, Derick and I had talked a few times about how we had never received any compensation for our work on the show, but I would always feel bad about going there, so I'd circle back to remind him that the show was a ministry, which is where the conversations always ended.

But tonight, with Pops in the room, Derick wanted to speak.

"I'm just wondering, Pops, do you think we could maybe see some kind of income from the show at some point?"

Pops stiffened. I cringed, braced for impact. He appeared shocked. When he regained his calm, he spoke cautiously.

"Derick, from the beginning, our family saw this as a ministry. An opportunity to show the world that children are a blessing. When we first launched this podcast, we made nothing from it. I was the one who was able to negotiate a favourable agreement for our family. I could retire today. "The only reason I'm still doing this is for you children."

Pops sat back. Question evaded. Conversation is over.

I looked at Derick. I could see he was thinking. It appeared as if he was double and triple-checking a computation column before pushing return. Finally, he spoke again.

"How about we get a certain percentage of what comes in?" Could that work?

Pops halted, his jaw set firmly. "We used to pay Josh, but decided not to do that after a while because it wasn't a very good idea." Then he shifted, smiling at each of us and altering the route, as if hunting for another way to shut things down. "Michelle is the one who had all these children. We wouldn't even have this show without her."

Pops clearly wanted us to follow his cues and leave this dance, but Derick refused. He was respectful, yet his tone was tough and unwavering. "That is correct, but we have also added a lot of value to the show and made significant contributions. After all, the show is titled "Jill and Jessa: Counting On."

It was a game of chess. I knew Derick could make other moves, such as mentioning that our wedding alone had drawn 4.4 million viewers for hours of prime-time television, or that as a couple, we'd participated in multiple People magazine cover shoots to promote both the wedding and Israel's birth episodes, both of which had been huge success stories.

Pops was quick to reply. "I know you produced some iPhone videos or something for the pregnancy and birth stuff, which we appreciate, but it takes a team effort. Everyone must pitch in. Some of the kids, for example, spend a lot of time photographing other aspects of their lives. And at times, some will be more involved than others, but it all balances out in the end."

For a time, I assumed Pops was finished with the topic. But he astonished me.

Turning to Derick, he inquired, "How much are you worth? Ten bucks per hour? Twelve? That is how much I pay some of my other employees."

It was the first time I'd heard of Pops paying someone in the family, but I could see the symptoms. It was not an invitation to debate or discuss, and it was definitely not a joke. It was a dismissal. He urged us to back off and go into full retreat. But Derick wouldn't have any of it.

"Well," Derick answered calmly, "what's the show worth?"

"Huh?"

"You can't determine the value of a worker to a business until you know how much the entire business is worth. So, before we tell you how much we're worth, we need to know what kind of arrangement you have with TLC."

Pops' mood worsened significantly. He was already upset, and his efforts to remain calm were beginning to show. "Derick, when we started this all those years ago, we just wanted to reach out and teach people that children are a blessing. It's not anything we were looking for. God provided us with this chance, and we believe he has blessed it by allowing us to reach so many people who would never have visited a church otherwise. Almost every day, we receive emails from people who say they have been affected. They've told us how witnessing Christian ideals shown on the show inspired them to commit their lives to Jesus, return to church, or have more children. Consider how many individuals we have been able to reach through a secular television network. I'm not saying your job here isn't excellent, but we reach more people through the show than you do on the mission field."

The sting was intense.

All the moment Pops and Derick were talking, I was wincing and trying to hide myself right there on the bed, wanting the conversation would end. All of my internal alarms against resisting authority were going out at high force. However, Pops' response was biting. It hurt. It felt like it was meant to make us back away.

But Derick didn't get scared easily.

I understand, Pops. But we would appreciate it if you could pray about potentially paying us something. Jill has devoted countless hours to filming over the last decade, but she has little to show for it financially. I know she's the first daughter to marry and you're still figuring it out, so we understand how hard it is, but I'm sure when the other kids get older and marry, they'll be wondering about these things as well."

When Pops left our room, Derick and I talked for a little longer, prayed, and went to bed. Derick had no trouble sleeping, but I was wired too tightly. I was frightened and panicked, and my heart was trying to leap out of my chest. I wasn't used to seeing someone respond and press Pops like that. I was concerned that we would be perceived as impolite, even though Derick had been nice throughout. Questioning a parent's authority was frowned upon in my culture, and I despised the idea of upsetting the balance. Nobody had ever done it before, but I was confident that if they did, the punishment would be harsh, most likely culminating in effective expulsion from the family. But, like Derick, I wanted to know more about the film's budget. So, long into the night, I peered into the darkness, hoping and praying that we might resolve things with Pops quickly and obtain additional information without causing any difficulties.

In the midst of those long, steamy hours, with the cicadas constantly singing outside, my thoughts drifted to Derick. He was not burdened by guilt or dread. It reminded me of Jesus' statement in the Bible about children not being scared to ask their father for bread.

I sensed a shift inside me. I was still mortified at the prospect of Pops being upset with us. But I was also proud of my hubby. He'd battled for his family, exactly like he promised when we married.

Pops and I got along OK for the rest of the mission trip. We had a fantastic time with some of my siblings who were old enough to accompany us on the vacation, and we hoped that Pops would do what we asked and pray about beginning to pay us and some of the other children.

Almost as soon as they left, the security situation in the area deteriorated. We heard tales of increasing gang activity and were cautioned that even strolling for a minute or two on our own down the wrong street would put us at risk of being kidnapped. We tried not to feed the worry, but we felt like we had a target on our backs, and the news that TLC had decided to take out ransom insurance on us only added to our concerns. Regardless of how much we tried to blend in and be a part of the community, we knew we were different. We were the only whites in the neighbourhood. It never troubled me when we visited as kids, but now that the threats are mounting and I, as a wife and mother, have so much more to lose, it feels different. People encouraged us to follow an unexpected schedule as much as possible, but that was difficult to do while remaining consistent in ministry.

In the end, they didn't come for us.

Almost every male in the country was in a gang, including youngsters as young as seven and eight. There were only two ways to get out: die or join a church. For whatever reason, the gangs ignored Christians, but only if they were truly committed to their church. Even still, the gangs required non-members to pay taxes or "rent" for their independence.

We had been attending and participating in many ministries at the local church linked with the ministry we were working with since we arrived, and we were making good friends with the folks there, particularly one family who lived ten minutes away. One of their daughters, Fatima, had a boyfriend who had left a gang. Raul was about sixteen or seventeen years old, and we occasionally saw him at church.

One day, while Raul was out on the street, a car pulled up and abducted him. No one ever saw or heard from him again. Everyone assumed the same two things: that someone, somewhere, had noticed that he hadn't been attending church regularly, and that Raul had died. Not long after, Fatima and her mother, Rosa, arrived at the church in tears. They explained that the group had advised them not to ask any questions or hunt for Raul or his body, because if they did, they would be next.

As the violence escalated, we decided to hire our own permanent guard, rather than just when the mission's personnel were present. It was another expense we couldn't afford, but the risk of not having someone armed to protect us was simply too high.

When we left Arkansas and returned to El Salvador in October, we informed Chad and everyone else of our promise to Mike to stay in the country until the end of July 2016. When Chad enquired about going to Houston for filming, we assumed he had forgotten, so we apologised for being unable to attend and reminded him that we had promised to stay in El Salvador.

He did not respond, but in January, Chad emailed us to say that he was ready to book tickets to Houston and needed to know which flight we preferred.

We wrote back, informing Chad that we would be unable to attend and reminding him of our agreement with Mike.

Chad's email response was polite but insistent. He said that the shoot was critical for the network's advertising of the show, and that our participation was essential. "It is a big deal for them," he wrote. "They've offered if you have a list of things you need from the States that you cannot get in CA, they will do that shopping for you and pack those things up to go back with you."

We responded swiftly, confirming our pledge to Mike. But we did say we would pray about it more and inform him that we would be speaking with Pops and Mom later that evening.

The next day, after chatting with my parents and praying, we went to bed. Our parents had been supportive, though it was evident that they wanted us to work something out with Chad and that the shoot was crucial. We returned to Chad the next day and informed him that we believed our time in the field was valuable and that we needed to honour our pledge, thus returning was not an option. We proposed that we film some footage and submit it to them, or that they have the crew travel down to meet us in a San Salvador airport hotel and shoot in front of a green screen in an afternoon. We hoped that we could work out a compromise.

We couldn't.

After numerous emails, Derick finally picked up the phone and phoned Chad. "We don't have to come back," he remarked. "Jill is not obligated to anything. Jill and I have only ever volunteered."

Chad responded, "Jill has a contractual obligation." "She must return."

"Excuse me?" Jill has never signed a contract.

The call ended shortly after, and Chad sent me an email describing what he said I was bound to do—a pasted list of various commitments to the show, including making ourselves accessible for all promotional efforts asked by the network. Chad's email mentioned a contract that I signed, which was fixed for five years.

I was perplexed.

Derick was suspicious. "Do you remember ever being part of any contract deals with the network?"

"No," I replied. "Never. Pops was always in charge of all network communications.

I was angered, bewildered, and deeply frightened by the prospect of there being some sort of true contract out there that may bind me to things beyond my control—a contract that I had no recall of ever signing.

While I was fretting about this phantom contract, attempts to persuade us to travel to Houston mounted over time. The phone calls and pressure increased, but we heard less from Chad and more from my parents. We begged Chad and Pops to provide us a copy of whatever contract we were bound to, but no one would give us anything. They basically continued pressing us about the shoot, saying that I was required to go.

The harder they pressed, the more we pushed back. The only promise I felt bound to was the one we had made to Mike to fully support the project.

The phone rang three days before the shoot. It was early in the morning, and I knew who was calling before I even looked at the screen. Pops had already called twice in the day.

Saying no to the Houston trip felt like pain, but Derick and I had been doing it for weeks and were determined to hold firm. After years of compromising and giving in to the network's demands, we had finally found a hill to die on. This was our opportunity to make a stand. We weren't trying to make things tough for the network or Pops. We wanted to make everybody happy. We wanted to work things out while still being as accommodating as possible. However, we felt compelled to make the right decision. Instead of being delighted or empowered, I was outraged that it had come to this. Angry and afraid.

"Pops…," I responded quickly as he started speaking. "That is not…" "That is not what we are saying."

The anxiety altered the tone of my speech. I felt younger, like if I were twelve rather than twenty-five. Maybe that's what he wanted, to put the perfect amount of pressure on the appropriate nerves. But I didn't want to cave and give in. I wanted Pops to understand why we were taking such a strong stand. I wanted him to understand that we had made a commitment to our ministry. I wanted dad to be proud of us, but all I heard was frustration.

"Your presence is critical in this situation. Jill and Jessa are Counting On, and they need you. "Surely Mike can spare you for a day?"

Derick approached and stood beside me, his arm across my shoulders. My heartbeat was racing. I felt nauseous.

I placed Pops on speakerphone so we could both hear what he was saying, but his request had remained the same in all of his previous calls. He wanted us to board a plane that weekend and arrive in Houston on time for the filming. But, while the request was the same, his tone differed. In all previous contacts, he had attempted to persuade us. Now he was trying to make us feel guilty.

"Is this you or is this Derick who is the problem here?"

I'd never heard Pops say anything like that before, and it hurt like a dagger to hear him try to push us against each other in that way. I was speechless.

"This is not like you, Sweet Jilly Muffin. Is Derick behind this? Are you struggling financially? "Are you depressed?"

I could feel Derick tense beside me.

"Pops," he murmured, his tone cool and controlled. "We're not trying to ruin anything. We wish we could help, but we have made a promise here."

There was a gap before Pops spoke. When he did, his voice became harder.

"If you don't come back for the filming, everything will go wrong. We've just gotten the show back up and running, and we need to be very careful not to upset the network. They cannot film the advertising material for Jill and Jessa: Counting On without you, Jill. Consider this: if you don't attend this shoot and TLC cancels the show again, everyone will look at you and know that it was your fault and that you could have prevented it. "Are you going to be okay carrying that burden?"

"Hey…," Derick defended me.

"Let me talk to you for a minute, Derick, because you are forcing your wife to break her word. Is that what you plan to do? Make her breach her promise? If this is the case, I must inform you that you are failing your family and leading them down a destructive path. Are you ready for that? Do you understand what happens if you breach a legally enforceable contract?"

It was the first time he addressed the contract other than via email, and we still hadn't received it. I could feel blood rushing to my face. I was very irritated.

There was a moment of stillness.

"You know," suggested Pops, "maybe you should flip a coin."

"Excuse me?" Derick asked.

"One coin. I did it when I was considering running for US Senate. I flipped it three times, and it came up heads each time. That's how I realised I needed to run."

Both of us sat silently. That appeared to aggravate Pops.

Let me tell you something right now! You're gonna be sued! You'll need every penny you have because you're going to be sued!"

Pops called back later the same day. And for the first time, we did not respond. We simply let the phone ring.

We performed the same thing on the next call.

And the next.

I felt a glimmer of relief, but it was overpowered by a deep sense of shame for disrespecting him in this way.

My mind was whirling, and my stomach was excruciatingly tight. Even on mute, the sound of the phone buzzing into life echoed the gunfire that had pushed us into hiding months before. I felt tense and anxious. There was no deep or dark closet in which I could hide at the moment.

Finally, we turned off the phones.

My anxiety simply grew worse.

All afternoon, I was in agony, alternating between fear and remorse every few seconds. I felt as if I were in labour, but not like I had been with Israel. This was not a new life I was bringing into the world, and there was no notion that if we could just get through the storm with Pops, everything would be fine. On the contrary, I was scared that things were going to get much worse.

Later, when it was dark and all we could hear outside were cicadas, I started crying. Derick was hugging me close, trying to make me feel safe and secure. But all I felt was fear and remorse. Guilt and fear. My own father did not recognize me. Did not like me. Perhaps he didn't even love me anymore.

What did I do?

What had I become?

"What if he's right, Derick?" I wailed in the dark. "What if we show up in America and we're taken to jail?"

Derick hugged me tightly, telling me everything will be fine.

"They're not going to sue the poor missionaries in Central America who have no contractual obligation and who haven't received so much as a cent in return for their work."

But the terror I felt was quite real. I was persuaded that by disobeying Pops in this way, by stepping out from under his protection, I was putting myself in grave danger. If the courts don't punish me, perhaps God will.

On the day of the filming, when my adult siblings were in Houston, I awoke feeling strange. Not entirely improved, but not as awful as before. Some of the guilt had subsided, and the terror wasn't as tight around my throat. I felt as though I could breathe again. We had made it all the way to Saturday and had not given up. For the first time in my life, I felt like I was advocating for myself.

Saturdays are often crowded in El Salvador, and this one was no exception. We always worked in a nearby hamlet with a lot of gang activity, arranging job skills training and leading a Bible study. Aside from that, Derick still needed to continue preparing for his Sunday lecture. It was fantastic to feel like we were doing something, and to be distracted.

I was just completed feeding Israel when I heard a car approaching out front. The automobile doors slammed shut, and a voice I could recognize anywhere shouted out.

"Hey! Derick? Jill? "Are you there?"

I opened the door and saw Mom and Pops walking down the stairs. Her eyes were teary. Pops was behind his phone, filming the family reunion.

I wasn't sure what to say. My Sweet Jilly Muffin mask was not showing on command. Derick, too, was stunned.

"We wanted to come and see you," Pops added after an uneasy moment. "Didn't we, Michelle?"

She nodded, and Pops put the phone aside. He glanced directly at me. I felt the barriers get closer, and I braced for contact.

"I realise I was a little harsh," he admitted. "I'm sorry for some of the things I said."

I reached for Derick's hand. If I ever needed a reminder that my spouse and I were one, it was now.

Chapter 6: No Agreement

In the first week of August 2016, we flew to northwest Arkansas. There was a lot to be grateful for, and a lot to ponder about. Derick and I were both relieved that we had been able to keep our promise to Mike, and we both felt we had left behind excellent friends and a growing ministry. Even though we only intended to return to the United States for two to three months, it was difficult to say goodbye. We were scheduled to attend two weddings—one for Derick's brother and the other for my sister Jinger—as well as a large amount of filming for the program. The weddings I was quite thrilled about. The filming, not so much. There were elaborate plans for the team to accompany us while we all prepared for the wedding, as well as document a slew of regular tasks, such as going to the grocery store, so that we could discuss all we'd missed while we'd been gone.

That final trip on the long journey home was far from settled. Israel was just a year old and wouldn't sit still for more than a few minutes at a time. Inside, I was just as restless. Just as uneasy. As we drew closer to home, I felt worse.

We have acquired a partial copy of the controversial contract cited by Chad a few months ago. Not the entire contract, but a few extracts, including a stipulation that required me to notify the network if I learned I was pregnant, as well as the final page with my and my siblings' signatures written in.

That signing sheet felt instantly familiar, especially when I saw the date I signed it.

June 20, 2014.

The day before Derick and I got married. The day before, Pops had told me that he had some easy documents for us all to sign in the dining room, and that it simply concerned how we would be paid— not that we'd ever been paid for any of our work.

I was upset when I found out, but now that we were returning to visit the family for the first time, I was more relaxed. However, I was still nervous.

The entire family was waiting for us. A film crew was also present, which made me wonder how genuine the embraces and "welcome backs" and "we love yous" were.

It turned out that they were genuine. Once the cameras had left and we were back at the Big House, it was as if the Houston shoot conflict had never occurred. I even began to believe—and hope—that Pops' apologies when he and Mom arrived that day was entirely genuine. We had not spoken much since then. Perhaps he'd see our point of view and be willing to discuss paying us fairly for our labour. Perhaps he realised the true significance of what we were doing in El Salvador and didn't have to constantly downplay its relevance in comparison to the show.

As a result, with each chat, shared meal, and time when I prepared for impact and wasn't chewed out by Pops, I could feel myself relaxing. There were still a lot of questions in my mind regarding the contract and why Pops had duped me into signing it, and I was still concerned about how he'd tried to put a rift between Derrick and me on that phone call. But I was fine leaving those for another day. We planned to spend the limited time we had at home relaxing before returning to the mission field to serve again.

It didn't take long for that peaceful situation to deteriorate. But the disruption had nothing to do with Pops or the concert. This wasn't even a terrible thing. What pushed our plans off track was entirely up to me and Derick. I became pregnant again.

In any other year, nothing would have changed. Derick and I would have cheerfully returned to El Salvador a few weeks later, knowing that the baby would thrive in my womb in Central America as well as in the United States. But 2016 was unlike any previous year. The Zika virus was spreading over Latin America, posing an even greater risk to women in the early stages of pregnancy.

Finally, due to filming responsibilities, including a commercial shoot in December that we were forced to attend, we had to wait until at least the end of the year before returning to El Salvador. Mike was nice and said he understood, and we agreed to return shortly after the filming. Aside from keeping Dillard baby number two healthy, it allowed us to be completely available for anything the show required. Even though my and Jessa's names were in the title, the presentation actually focused on several of us older kids. Jana, John-David, Joseph, Josiah, Joy, and Anna were all featured alongside us, and with Jinger engaged to Jeremy and another wedding on the horizon, we weren't as prominent as we had been in the first few seasons of Counting On. After thirteen years of filming—nearly half my life—I was finally beginning to envision a future without it.

Derick and I appreciated having time and space to discuss, imagine, and pray about what our life would be like after we finished our second year in El Salvador. We had enjoyed being a part of the mission project, but our time was drawing to a close. At the same time as our baby was developing discreetly inside me, we began to make plans for what we might do next in our lives.

Pops' text arrived early one October morning, to a group of older children. Pops was always sending messages to various members of our family—those who lived at the Big House, those who were older, those who were younger (but not the smallest), married children, and single children—but being summoned to a family meeting was triggering. The wounds from the previous few I had attended were still raw.

When Pops started talking about Josh, everything sounded so familiar.

"He's had a few more struggles," Pops explained when everyone had sat down and the door was closed. "Y'all already know that Josh has recently got his own car lot, and so we feel like it's best for him to go out on his own now."

Pops stopped. His comments were often ambiguous, with the intention of discouraging rather than encouraging debate. So, while we could have asked a lot of questions, no one said anything. Our primary role in these family sessions was usually to listen. Substantial issues were not discussed.

But it turned out that the meeting was not about Josh at all.

"Anyway," Pops smiled, "Mom and I have been discussing, and some of the boys are becoming older and might use some money to help them go on with their lives. And we felt it would be a good idea for you to have some money so you could accomplish what you needed to do in life. We want to offer you each $80,000, and I'm guessing some of you will use it to establish businesses, buy homes, or do whatever you need to get started."

The room erupted into a chorus of surprise and gratitude. In my entire life, I had never been more surprised by what Pops said.

"You know," he added when the room became quieter, "you can thank Derick for this. He's been speaking with me about paying some of you."

Everyone else dismissed the comment as meaningless. But for Derick and me, sitting side by side, it was a trigger. I was delighted Pops had finally decided to pay something outright to some of the kids, and I was glad he recognized Derick's role in the process, but my thoughts wandered back to the steamy bedroom where we'd sat with Pops before Christmas, Derick looking perplexed and frustrated. Pops seems enraged. I felt like I was in a world of trouble. As the plane approached the ground, I braced myself for collision.

I suppressed my emotions and grabbed for my husband's hand. I gave him three squeezes and received four in return, then waited to see what else Pops had to say about Derick and me.

He did not.

"All I'll need is for you to sign anything. I am currently in the process of preparing documents. I will bring you the money once you have signed."

As soon as we were alone, Derick expressed precisely what I was thinking.

"I don't get it. It raises a lot of questions. Why 80,000? "Why now?"

"So, what is it for? Is this compensation for the shows we've already performed, or is it a gift?"

We spoke late into the night and got nothing. We were frustrated to be left with so many questions and just Pops to answer them. And, given recent experience, we didn't feel comfortable asking him all of our questions anyhow. A debate can simply leave us with no real facts and extra grief. Maybe Pops was just being generous, but we both suspected he was playing some sort of game. After all, thirteen years as a filming family had taught us that everything comes at a cost. Plus, Pops' lifestyle alone indicated that the show had generated far more than the equivalent of $80,000 per.

Initially, the alterations were subtle. We'd received more costly gifts for Christmas, better RVs to transport us together, and I'd observed when Pops began making larger and more generous donations to those in need. However, as the show grew, Pops was able to purchase an increasing number of rental homes. He continued to be kind, frequently letting friends and relatives use numerous of his residences at reduced prices or even for free.

It took a few days for the mist to dissipate, and we began to believe that the money was not a simple gift.

First, Pops mentioned that none of us should discuss the money with anybody else, either inside or outside the family: "If you have any issues, don't stir contention among the brethren," he urged. "You come to me."

A few weeks later, the papers arrived—a four-page agreement emailed over by Chad. After being duped into signing the prior contract, Derick and I took extra precautions to examine this one and showed it to a lawyer, along with the portions of the previous agreement we'd received. If we were going to sign Pops' new contract, we wanted to be certain about what we were giving up.

The contract was not with TLC or any other network. It was with Mad Family Inc., a corporation Mom and Pops had previously established. In exchange for the $80,000, we agreed to make not only ourselves, but also our children and any future children, available to any show created or participated in by Mad Family Inc. for the next seven years—plus an unlimited number of years beyond that if the company chose. We would be paid for that labour as well, but at a fixed amount that we would have to accept without discussion. We would also have to sign an NDA, which would be valid for the rest of our life. Eighty thousand dollars was a lot of money, but the cords were tight enough to suffocate.

Derick and I didn't need to have a discussion. Neither of us were going to sign. Not that we informed Chad or Pops straight away. We decided to avoid saying no to Pops unless absolutely necessary.

Pops had made it clear that we were not to discuss the bargain with anybody else, including ourselves, our other siblings, or anyone outside the family. At the time, I thought Pops' level of secrecy and control over us was usual. We had been trained to follow, and it would not have occurred to me to see the hypocrisy in the fact that he would caution us against causing division among the brethren while also manipulating us against one another and duping us into signing agreements.

Most were afraid of Pops' wrath and obeyed, but not everyone did. A few siblings inquired if we were going to sign. I told them no, selecting my words carefully to avoid causing family problems. I was shocked that practically everyone I spoke with felt comfortable signing. Some stated that they wanted to make some changes to the agreement first, but I began to feel as if they were being carried away by a soon-to-be dangerous torrent. I wanted to rush in and save them, but I wasn't sure I had the power.

A few weeks later, we were on a Duggar family trip to Branson, Missouri, for Thanksgiving, when everything changed. A month had gone since we were given the contract to sign, and Derick and I had spent a lot of time discussing and praying about all that had happened recently, trying to find out how we might better communicate with Pops. After consulting with an attorney outside the family circle of influence, Derick and I decided that the next step would be to request that Pops send over a full copy of the contract that he had me sign the day before our wedding. He had already sent us a portion of it in June, but viewing the entire thing seemed like an excellent opportunity for him to be truthful and open with us. He resisted. At the very least, he was playing the same stalling game on the 2014 contract as we were on Pops' $80,000 one. But on vacation, when we weren't crammed on top of each other as we were at home, we had the opportunity to talk to Pops face to face.

We were seated at a table in an unoccupied area of Fritz's Adventure, a children's climbing facility in Branson, Missouri, when Pops approached and sat down.

"I feel like there's still something between us," he told me. There was a pause. Derick and I stared at each other.

"Well, yes," replied Derick. "There's been some trust broken recently that might take a while to rebuild."

"It goes both ways. "You've also broken my trust."

His stare was unwavering. I could taste bile in my throat. I thought that things were about to get ugly again.

Then Pops shocked me. "I'm sorry," he replied. I hadn't heard him say it many times before. The words sounded foreign. But I liked them.

I waited until he finished his sentence.

"I'm sorry that I didn't let you know what you were obligated to."

"But Jill never read the contract she was signing, so she wasn't obligated to anything," Derick explained, trying hard not to get frustrated. "Will you admit that?"

Pops shrugged. "Yes, okay. I apologise for forcing her to agree to something she was not required to."

"Thanks, Pops," I replied. "We forgive y'all and love y'all too and really hope we can move forward and have great family relationships."

Later, when everyone was sharing their gratitude, I was at a loss for words. I was thankful for Mom and Pops. I was grateful for my spouse, my son, and the small life growing in my womb. But most importantly, I wanted to express my gratitude to my husband for his bravery and courage despite the challenges we encountered together that year. Despite the stress of family life, he was my biggest supporter, and we were working together to reclaim control of our lives, one tiny decision at a time.

As the end of the year approached, we felt more pressure to sign the deal. We discussed it, prayed about it, and slept on it a lot. However, despite Chad and Pops' persistence and persuasiveness, we were unable to reach an agreement. Yes, we wanted the money—even though it was far from adequate recompense for the hours, days, and years spent filming—but we did not want to be bound by any legal commitment with Pops to obtain it.

Pops must have felt the same way, for he paid us a visit at home in the final days of December. I wanted to hide. I just wanted everything to go away. I did not want to have to pour concrete around my heart in order to protect myself from the blast.

But Pops was not there to fight. He was there to hand over a check for the whole $80,000. "What about the agreement?" Derick asked.

"I know you've been thinking about the contract and talking with Chad about modifications, and we had intended to get it all tied up by the end of the year, but we can continue those discussions. Mom and I spoke about it, and we really want to send you your payment right away. "We really love you guys."

"Thank you, Pops," I responded. I meant it, but I didn't rejoice. Somehow, it did not feel like the end of the story.

Pops had already approached another law company, but they declined to take on the case. Now, in February 2017, time was against us. The statute of limitations was approaching, and we needed to file by May. If we couldn't find a legal firm to hire us, our window of opportunity would close forever. What made it even more difficult was that none of us could afford to pay for it, despite Pops' $80,000 "gift." He offered to lend us the money, but I didn't feel right about being in debt to him. So we needed a firm capable of taking on local government, elected politicians, and a national media organisation on a contingency basis. It was a tough task, but thanks to a contact from my new brother-in-law, Jeremy, we located a firm in Los Angeles that believed we had a good enough case and was ready to take a chance on us.

When Pops heard, he called me. The muscle memory was strong, and I braced for impact, concerned that he would be furious that we had not included him or Chad in the process. However, his voice was calm and his remarks genuine. "I'm extremely proud of you all. "I'm so glad you found someone."

I sighed with relief.

"But," he continued, "I would be really cautious about how you handle all of this. You know, we just started the program back up."

Okay, Pops. "I love you."

I was concerned about the show. I was worried about Pops, too. I didn't want to disrupt the fragile and feeble harmony that was developing between us. But I was happy that my sisters and I have our own counsel to aid us with this. LA was a long way from Arkansas, and for once, I was convinced that Pops would be unable to exert control over the situation. Finally, we could defend ourselves.

Soon after we returned to El Salvador, we received a call from the International Mission Board, or IMB, with whom we had a job interview at a missionary expo—the same organisation with which Derick had previously worked and with which we had made contact shortly after our honeymoon. Their process was slow, and we had to be a member of their church denomination for three years. With that hurdle crossed, we began to have more in-depth discussions about working with them.

The fact that we were already well-known through the show undoubtedly made a lot of organisations cautious about drawing too much attention to their delicate work, so they passed us over, but the IMB was eager to look into us. And, while being well-known meant that some of our job opportunities inside this organisation would be limited, we were thrilled. It felt as if we'd discovered gold. We liked everything about them—their purpose, their principles, the way they functioned and supported their missionaries—and were overjoyed when they extended the earlier invitation to join them. They sent missionaries all throughout the world, and they advised us to visit Spain or Panama.

Starting work with Mike following our initial interview had been very simple—all we needed to do was agree on the scope of the work, hammer out a few specifics like money and housing, and book our flights—but with IMB, things were a little different. It was far larger, had been around for 150 years, and the measures we had to take were far more complicated. There were training classes to attend, vetting procedures to complete, and interviews with potential mission partners to do. On average, it took between two and four years to be accepted as a missionary and sent out onto the mission field. We had been working on it for a while and were eventually declared virtually ready. Finally, we were able to allow ourselves to be excited about the upcoming new chapter.

The call was mostly standard, but one question threw us off guard.

"We just want to double check, is there anything that you guys can and can't do with the whole filming thing you do with your family, Jill?"

"You mean contractually?" "I said."

"Yeah. Do you have any formal agreements that limit your ability to fully dedicate yourself to your work?"

Derick and I held hands out of sight of the camera.

"Well, yes," he started. "There is an agreement Jill was tricked into signing the day before our wedding, but we don't feel obligated to it morally or legally because of the way the signature was gained."

There was a moment of stillness. The man we were chatting to seemed perplexed.

Derick looked at me. "We're happy to cut ties with anything filming related though, aren't we?"

I nodded. "We're ready to do that."

Following this, I said, "We will quit the show right now to show you that we're serious about working with you."

"Well, okay then." The guy smiled. "That's excellent. If you can supply us with evidence proving you are free of any contracts, that would be ideal."

It was awkward to discuss quitting the show with someone other than Derick. We'd been talking about it for about a year, and the timing seemed appropriate. However, knowing that our secret had been revealed to the world felt odd. It felt dangerous. It felt freeing, too.

All of our whispered chats about when we should leave the event seemed to go forever. Now that we had decided to go, we needed to figure out how we were going to do so. We did not have the luxury of time when making that selection. We needed to press on and get things moving so that we could be released from the show in time to begin our new position on the mission field in the coming year.

We wrote two versions of the email. The first was a short and straightforward resignation letter emailed to everyone we could think of at TLC and Discovery, the parent channel, and the production business. We offered them a deadline of May 31, 2017, and stated that we will be back in Arkansas in mid-May and available to conduct any filming they requested. We didn't replicate Pops or Chad because we wanted to portray that we were capable adults who could make decisions and interact with the network on our own, as well as walk out as cleanly and without interference as possible.

The second email we wrote to Chad.

We just wanted to let you know that after much thought and prayer, we have decided to walk away from the show. We believe that as of the end of May 2017, we are no longer permitted to participate in any capacity on the show.

We read and reread them both till I could say them in my sleep. We had a lengthy discussion about what might happen once we sent them. We discussed staying within our comfort zone and doing what we knew was right. We talked until there was nothing more to say.

I felt afraid. I was so afraid that I began to have contractions. I was twenty-nine weeks pregnant and had just begun my third trimester.

All I could do was breathe and trust that everything would turn out okay.

We thought at the last minute that calling my parents first, rather than emailing them, would be more appropriate and considerate. So we prayed, took up the phone, and called my parents while holding back tears and my stomach in knots. They were both on the call. As we informed them of our decision to stop filming at the end of May, tears streamed down my pregnant abdomen and soaked the blouse that covered it. I expected a difficult reaction or disagreement, as we had in the past, but it did not occur. We kept the call short. They remained cool and did not ask any questions. They did not say much, but thanked us for informing them.

After hanging up, we sent the emails and waited.

The fallout was immediate. Chad emailed back, demanding to know who else we had sent the email to. TLC also responded by email, expressing an interest in speaking with me. We informed them we'd be pleased to speak with them and provide our side of the story. We wanted to explain how we had been unaware of some aspects of the contract. They first agreed, but Chad must have heard about the call because they included him in the email thread—and the network was no longer authorised to speak with us unless Chad was also on the call.

From that point on, it was Groundhog Day: the same struggle over and over. We struck a brick wall every time we tried to get TLC to provide us with documentation proving we were released from the contract. We still had just a partial copy of the June 2014 contract, and neither Chad nor Pops would give us the entire document. Meanwhile, we were left trying to persuade the IMB that the months-long wait was merely temporary and that we would eventually have the legal release they sought. The only thing that seemed to be going right was my pregnancy. The anxiety-inducing contractions had only lasted a day or so and had not escalated to labour.

We attempted to make the most of our remaining weeks in El Salvador. Despite all of the Duggar-family drama and show-related craziness that we had witnessed during our time there, we felt strongly connected to the people we had worked with. I had grown particularly close to the pastor's wife, Maria. She was the sweetest, and I knew she would be there for me whenever I needed it. Leaving her and everyone else was going to be difficult, especially since the security situation had deteriorated even further in recent months.

Our former guard, German, was another person we would miss the most. We'd known him for a while, and he was always willing to translate and make people laugh. His wife created the greatest chocolate, which we used to buy whenever we wanted a treat. He said his favourite meal was the hamburgers we cooked for him. German had been a member of MS-13, one of the vicious gangs responsible for much of the violence in El Salvador. He had become a Christian and attended church on a regular basis, but this wasn't enough to keep his past from catching up with him. There were whispers that he was a target, and that if he continued to work with us, we would also become targets.

It was difficult, but we realised we needed to let German go. We stayed in touch after he ceased working as our security, and he visited us several times with his family.

We received word one month before our scheduled return to the United States that a German had been slain.

Derick and I were shocked and devastated.

All of the upheaval and trauma that the show had brought into our lives was nothing compared to Germany's murder. We were aware of the hazards when we began our work in El Salvador, but I never imagined the danger would come this close to us.

The despair seemed to hang over the entire valley.

For weeks, I felt empty inside.

There was also frustration. We had been unable to obtain any documents verifying our release from the performance, and the IMB could only wait so long. They underlined to us that unless something changed with the contract deal during the following several months, we risked losing the job opportunity we had been looking for in Panama.

Nevertheless, there was optimism. Our second child was thriving inside me, unconcerned about anything else going on in the world that might be bothering either of us. I was over thirty-three weeks pregnant, and everything seemed to be going well for the last few weeks. Despite all of the tension and uncertainty around our future, Mom and Pops and I agreed on one thing: the new life we were about to bring into the world was nothing short of a blessing.

With no job lined up and no idea whether we'd ever be able to get out of the contract, we worked hard to stay cheerful. Our baby, a boy, was due six weeks after we arrived, and we would spend most of our time before then preparing for my sister Joy's approaching wedding or filming our final interviews for the show.

Of course, someone from the program asked whether we were willing to have cameras present when I went into labour.

We didn't have to think twice about replying to them.

"Absolutely. "No way," we said on several occasions.

Chad threw us a genuine curveball, though. He notified us that he was no longer able to work with Dillard Family Ministries and was stepping down from our board. That surprised neither of us, which was a comfort. What bothered us was when we checked the balance of the ministry bank account. Chad had withdrawn practically everything, leaving us with only a few hundred dollars in the ministry account, which we used to pay ourselves a salary. We approached him, and he told us a story about a CPA bill that was due, despite the fact that his salary was intended to cover those fees.

The whole thing tasted unpleasant. Perhaps we would have battled harder on another day. But, with so much on our plates and the future so uncertain, neither of us felt like fighting another battle. We just wanted to get through the next stage in our life. There was only one last loose end to tie off before we were free. The show.

The producers asked if we could set aside five hours to shoot some final exit interviews with us, which they could use to inform viewers of our decision to quit the show. It seems funny today, but I don't recall much from the last interviews we did for Jill & Jessa: Counting On. I remember how I felt—a mix of sorrow and thankfulness, relief and fear, happiness that this was all behind us while also wondering what would come next—but I don't recall what we said. They asked us to give them several versions of our decision to leave the show. I don't think any of it made the final cut of the show. Part of me still wonders why they didn't explain to the audience why we departed. Part of me understands that it didn't matter.

Aside from that, I don't recall anything that marked the end of our engagement in the show. There were no speeches and no final papers to finish. We had just completed answering the question, and the room was silent for a little moment.

"That's it," the cameraman stated.

We rose up from the couch where we'd been interviewed hundreds of times before, in the shop building turned studio at the front of the Big House grounds. Nobody from my family was present, so after saying our goodbyes to the film crew, we simply walked back to our car and drove home.

That was it.

For us, the show had ended. We were out. Returning to the mission field was more difficult than we had anticipated, but at least we were now free to do whatever we wanted. Free to relocate, to create our lives the way we wanted them to be built, and to raise our sons without the obstacles that I had encountered. Part of me was thrilled. Part of me found it scarier than anything I'd ever seen. I felt confused and unsure about this new world ahead of me, as if I had been unexpectedly liberated from a life sentence. It was all too big. All too unknowable. I was just twenty-six years old.

Derick hugged me close those evenings, squeezing the skin so tightly across my abdomen that you could see the outline of the little foot or elbow on the other side.

"You see," Derick explained anytime our kid in utero kicked and squirmed. "Everything's going to be alright."

Chapter 7: Pushed Aside

2017 finished on a sour note.

2018 started badly.

We received word from the missionary organisation where we hoped to serve. They'd been waiting over a year for us to submit legal proof that we were no longer obligated by the contract I signed the day before my wedding day. Despite repeatedly asking Pops, Chad, and the network for a release or at least a full copy of the contract itself, we still had nothing to show them other than Chad's typed-up bullet points informing us that the contract ran "for five years" until June 2019, and Pops' partial contract pages, which did not provide us with all of the information we required. We'd lost our job in Panama, and they'd kept us on their reserve list for as long as they could, but time was up. If we ever became available and wanted to serve with them, we'd have to reapply and go through the entire procedure again, which would take years.

We were devastated. The mission field had been the only place I felt free, and I was certain that we were meant to serve there. We'd already waited a year, and with Pops refusing to comply, we'd have to wait another year and a half before even considering breaking out of the contract and working with the mission organisation, assuming they'd accept us again. Neither Derick nor I felt comfortable putting our lives on hold for so long.

I was upset. A while later, I told my mother about losing my job, and Pops ultimately found out. We were together one evening when he mentioned it.

"You should have told me," he replied. "I'm sure we could have worked something out."

I bit my lip so hard I thought I'd draw blood.

"No, Pops," Derick replied. "That isn't the point." You are not entitled to know what is going on in our life. What would have been most beneficial would have been to advocate for us with TLC, explain everything to them, and get us removed from the contract."

Around the same time, he texted us, finally providing us with a little but critical piece of the puzzle: the day the contract expired.

It wasn't 2019, after all. It was June 2018.

We were both astonished and upset. Our future has been impacted once more by a lack of openness, with Pops acting on a need-to-know basis. If we had known about the contract's expiration date, the mission organisation might have held on a little longer. If Pops had been more open with us early, we might have been able to resume our task without delay. And maybe if we had told Pops about everything that had been going on with the IMB earlier, he would have helped sooner, but neither of us wanted to give him that much control over our lives, or risk him making direct contact with the IMB and attempting to use his influence to persuade them to bend the rules for us. We wanted to stand on our own two feet.

For a while, we pondered contacting the organisation again to see whether this new information altered anything, but we opted not to. We still lacked real proof and complete information—no contract, just a text message. Derick had taken the LSAT and applied to law school, and he had just learned that he had been accepted. We believed that some legal training would be advantageous to both of us in the future. The lawsuit my sisters and I filed against the people who had published the investigation was still in its early stages. In Touch had filed a successful motion to be dismissed from the lawsuit, and we were learning that as "public figures," we weren't afforded the same level of protection as "private figures," though we still hoped to prove intentional mishandling of juvenile records later on, which could bring them back into the suit. The city and county, as well as their defendants, were filing appeals on portions of their claims, but things were still moving along, slowly but steadily.

We attempted to put the termination of our IMB ambitions behind us, but after Easter, things flared up again. Derick had been making comments on Twitter, expressing his opinions on various topics and making a few enemies. It earned him a quiet talk with Pops, as well as a warning. "Be careful," he warned. "If you've got problems, come to me."

Initially, neither of us felt inclined to accept his offer. We'd tried it previously, and it didn't go well. Instead, we did our best to swallow our irritation and avoid doing anything that might irritate Pops. But when the problems persisted, we decided it was best not to just brush things under the rug and keep pretending. We decided to accept Pop's advice and approach him with our troubles, but not in person this time. Based on our recent past and the desire for a little buffer, we decided to write our ideas down in a letter.

We spent days working on it. We worked hard to ensure that it was straightforward and without too much emotion. We simply wanted to list everything that had upset us so that Mom and Pops had the best opportunity of knowing where we were and how we felt.

What began as a page or two gradually grew. We wrote paragraph after paragraph of issues we genuinely wanted to fix. We were exhausted by the end of the letter, which was twenty-seven pages long. Instead of sleeping on it or reviewing it, we chose to deliver it exactly as it was. Besides, we were on a family trip to Texas with Derick's outreach program, so it felt like the perfect opportunity to have a little extra physical distance between us.

We were relieved and perplexed when Pops emailed back a brief response, not answering the questions we'd posed, but apologising for "all of the ways that my actions & controlling spirit & lack of sensitivity & lack of communication have hurt you and Jill." He thanked us for bringing it to his attention, asked for prayer, and begged our forgiveness, saying he loved us very much.

Then, as summer began, we arrived home one day to find a letter. And that's when everything fell apart.

Derick reviewed his spreadsheet again. "About a hundred and thirty thousand dollars more."

We followed up with Pops' CPA via email, asking him to explain two things: how Pops came up with the $80,000 figure in the first place, and why there was such a big gap between that and what we declared on our returns. We had waited years for a copy of the contract and were still waiting, so neither of us had high hopes for a prompt or detailed response.

His response did arrive quickly, but I believe the CPA was unaware of most of it, since his responses appeared to indicate that he believed we were aware of more than we were.

Pops wasn't offering much assistance, either. Though he did avoid the question and give us some unsolicited advice:

"It's important not to live off your life savings but to reinvest it," he told me. "Jason bought a house, fixed it up, and is now selling it. You could do the same. Instead of paying rent, buy a house and fix it up; this will save you money and boost your savings.

He also stated that he had seen a "spirit of ungratefulness" inside us. It was evident to me that he did not appreciate our questioning his financial judgments. Normally, he'd have been a little smoother, attempting to win us over. But now he sounded like he'd had enough, like we'd tried his patience and he couldn't wait for the emails to end and us to stop asking questions so he could go on. Derick tried delicately to explain that if we did have income, we wanted to tithe on it. He said that he had already paid the taxes and tithed our half. Pops said that if we wanted to tithe on our income, he would have to kick some of the families he was giving free rent out of their homes. What we wanted most was transparency and to find out why I hadn't been paid the amount stated to the government.

Pops replied with a question of his own.

"Derick. What amount do you think you and Jill are owed?"

It was not intended to be a question that required an answer. It seemed like a challenge. As our emails with Pops continued, it felt as if he was daring us to speak a number, to show him disrespect. It wasn't like him to be so harsh, and I wasn't used to feeling such coldness radiating from him. I loved Pops but despised the battle, so part of me wanted to quit. I questioned if it was even worth fighting. I simply wish we could handle this civilly and without getting too emotional.

The Fourth of July was approaching, and for the first time, Derick and I decided not to attend the yearly celebrations at a friend's house, where I knew my parents would be present. It felt like a significant decision, and we needed to make some space between ourselves. I was hoping that if we could just give some space and let things simmer down a little, things would get better.

A spell of silence was not my only thought. First, I asked Mom and Pops if they would be willing to meet with a mediator to assist us resolve some of our concerns in a constructive manner. They agreed, even saying they'd be pleased for us to choose the mediator and schedule the meeting. I appreciated it and hoped that after a few weeks, we'd all be able to get down and figure things out.

My idea encountered a setback early on. I had asked my church to propose some people to help facilitate the meeting, and they had given me three names of people who could sit with us all and mediate. Finding a time when they could all make work was challenging, so it was reduced to just two of the three options. Then, in August, Derick began law school, adding to the pressure on our life and schedule. Finally, we agreed on a date for the first week of October, but the other mediator had to withdraw at the last minute, leaving only one.

I hadn't seen Pops in three months or gone to the Big House at all. It was strange, and I felt separated from my family, but staying away was simpler than spending time with everyone and pretending everything was normal.

I felt worried when we arrived at the church for our meeting. We arrived early and spoke briefly with a friend of Derick's from the school of ministry, who was waiting outside. She had tattoos and a nose piercing, but I could tell she loved the show. When the mediator arrived, we went inside to wait for Mom and Pops.

When Pops entered the door, he smiled widely. As we exchanged awkward pleasantries and embraces, Pops extended his phone.

"Look at this," he stated.

Derick, the mediator, and I pushed in to watch as Pops hit play on a video he had just recorded. It was the girl from outside, and her smile was even wider than Pops'. She was describing how her previous life had been full of sin, but that watching the show had helped her change. She'd started wearing skirts and enrolled in the school of ministry to be near the Duggars. And now, to meet Pops and Mom in person, it was a wonderful day for her.

"Isn't that great?""Pops asked, his eyes wide and gleaming as he glanced at each of us. "She's so sweet."

It wasn't anything new. Pops had been capturing videos of anyone he met who complimented him on the program and how it had made a great impact on their life ever since he got a smartphone, and he'd share them with the rest of the family via group messaging. To him, it was a means to encourage people and serve as a reminder of the ministry's purpose. In the past, I would probably have agreed. But this time, it hurt to see him compliment the girl with the tattoos and the nose ring. How could he have an issue with my wearing jeans and getting my nose pierced while seemingly ignoring what this female had done to her body?

I brushed it off and attempted to concentrate.

Derick and I had come prepared, and I looked through the notes on my phone for topics we wanted to address.

It is not sinful for a woman who fears the Lord to wear slacks, wear a nose ring, or cut her hair.

That Pops wasn't merely disorganised or forgetful when he made me sign the contract without viewing it. It was a planned deceit.

We want Pops to be completely honest, including sharing the 2014 contract with us and informing us of any other agreements that affect us.

Pops can set things right by paying the full amount indicated by his accountant on my tax filings. Total: $130,249.98.

When Derick and I talked in the days and weeks preceding this meeting, those four items sounded like the most fundamental things we wanted to agree on. They looked logical and achievable at the time, and I imagined how great it would feel to have resolved them all. But sitting in the room, with the mediator introducing himself and thanking us all for our attendance, and Pops appearing confident and powerful, as if nothing in the world could ever affect him, I felt something different.

So, when the mediator asked me to speak first, I set the four points aside and tried to offer something that I believed would be helpful.

"I'm sorry it took so long for this meeting to happen," I said. My voice shook slightly, and I could feel my lungs stutter. "There have been some extremely unpleasant things that have happened, and we wanted to clear it all up. To have an excellent conversation together. We love you all, and I'm sure we all hope to be able to rebuild family bonds soon."

Pops' body language had changed since we chatted. He was no longer cheerful after seeing the video and seeing the girl outdoors. Instead, he sat motionless, lips rigid and gaze set in a stone-sculpted scowl.

"That letter you guys sent us." He paused, as if he were lost and didn't know where to proceed. He stared at Mom. She stared at me.

There was no scowl on her face, nor were her arms folded. Only a look of pain. The anguish of a mother torn by her baby.

"It was the most disrespectful thing I've ever read."

Her voice was gentle, but her words struck me harder than anything she had ever said to me.

I knew she was right; she was telling the truth. I wasn't sure how I'd messed up, but I knew I had. I had injured her and Pops, and it was never my aim.

I overheard Derick try to explain that we never intended for the letter to be interpreted that way. I looked at Pops. He still scowled.

"I'm sorry," I replied. "We love you and wish we had been more careful. We drafted the letter together and hoped it would help clarify our feelings. However, we kept adding to it until we were fatigued and decided to send it along.

My voice trailed off as I attempted to find the perfect words. But Pops was not listening to me. He had his own list of topics he wanted to talk about.

"Jill, you sent me a text message. You claimed I was verbally abusing you. I was also insulted by that. You know in your heart that's not right. Will you apologise for that?"

I am nervous now. I remembered sending the message in the hopes that it would alert Pops to how awful things had gotten, and that he would allow us some space to settle down. I'd written about not wanting to be verbally assaulted, and it was precisely how I felt at the moment. I had felt it in El Salvador as well. I wasn't sure if I could apologise for that. I looked at Derick as I remained silent.

Pops must have understood what I was thinking, because he stood up abruptly. "Are you not going to apologise?" Really?"

His voice was powerful, and it had an edge that I hadn't heard before. The moderator was pallid and was trapped on mute. Derick tensed, and I could tell he was about to step in. I squeezed his hand, hoping he received the message.

Hold back.

Please be quiet.

Do not allow this to get any worse than it already is.

We were seated in a horseshoe shape, the moderator in the centre, and the Dillards and Duggars facing each other from opposing couches, with an open space between us. Pops took a stride toward me, closing the distance.

It was hardly a gesture of reconciliation.

It was an act of hostility.

He towered over me, his entire body filled with rage. My face turned red. My eyes filled with tears.

Then there was a long, dreadful silence, which I wanted to fill but couldn't yet.

Derick's hand shook in mine, and I clutched harder than I'd ever squeezed, eager for him to stop talking.

"You understand why you are crying, don't you?" Your conscience is speaking to you. "That is why."

Pops' voice sounded so loud in my ears. His words were like strikes. I instantly sought to protect myself by blocking him out. I curled up in my seat, hoping to find safety in some sort of foetal position.

"You're guilty!" Pops was yelling, stabbing his finger at me, and standing directly over me.

Mom began crying.

Derick attempted to speak, but I pulled him back.

"You want to know why I'm crying?" My voice cracked and my eyes burned. "It's that you believe I'm an awful person because I wear jeans and have a nose ring, but you applaud that girl outside. That's why I am crying, Daddy. I am maturing and changing, just like that girl out there, but you cannot see it. You treat me as if I've abandoned you. "You treat me worse than you do my pedophilic brother."

Pops appeared surprised. He muttered, "Well...," I wondered if he was ready to agree with me and affirm that my disobedience was just as awful as Josh's.

But eventually, the moderator spoke out. "I think we should take a break."

The mediation meeting lasted three hours. Three hours of heated words, tears from both my mother and me, and little resolve. We didn't even get to inquire about the financial position or other topics we had planned to explore. By the end, my head was pounding and my heart felt raw. It was nearly tough to concentrate, but I clearly heard what the mediator said to Derick and me after Mom and Pops had left.

"You need professional help."

We agreed and started looking for a therapist immediately away. We soon located someone—we'll call him Mr. Ray McIntosh—a silver-haired professional Christian therapist with availability on his calendar. Derick was all in from the time we arranged our first appointment, but I had some baggage to deal with.

"A therapist is just someone you're paying to be your friend." I had heard it many times as a child, and it was stuck in my head. Pops continually warned us not to talk to anyone outside the family about anything related to the program or the family. "They may not comprehend. And they might not be consistent with IBLP teachings."

It was the old umbrella of protection, and I was scared of thinking for myself.

I was starting to dislike how the IBLP umbrella principle continued to affect me, much like the aftermath of a nuclear explosion. I despised how powerful it remained in my life, despite my several attempts to overcome it. I despised the fact that I still had to deal with it. I hoped I could sort things out, and I was tired of the emotional toll it was taking. I needed help, but I was afraid of becoming one of those individuals who relied on the world to solve their issues rather than God.

It wasn't entirely horrible. Samuel's eighteen-month checkup, which would reveal if he had experienced any long-term brain damage at birth, came at the worst possible time. The results, according to the neurologist, were conclusive: there was no evidence of any birth-related brain injury. It was a rare bit of good news, and I was overjoyed for days.

I was prepared to chat when we arrived at our first therapy session. The words poured out of both of us, as our therapist sat and listened, occasionally steering us back on track.

Ray announced his conclusion at the season's end. "I've attempted group mediation sessions previously, and they're quite difficult to complete. It's difficult to maintain control of the room, and it can quickly devolve into a yelling match."

"Yeah," I responded, my thoughts rushing back to me curled up on the chair, Pops jabbing a finger in sync with his ranting, and our first mediator sitting silently and astonished.

"I would propose that you consult a therapist, whether it is me or someone else, for a few sessions. Your parents can also visit someone else, and when you're ready, you may sign a document allowing the two therapists to talk and act as a liaison for a while. Perhaps you can ultimately meet with your parents, but I wouldn't advocate it.

It sounded fantastic, and we discussed it with Mom and Pops. To their credit, they phoned the other therapist recommended by Mr. McIntosh and met for a session. But the more time we spent in therapy, the more we realised we were a long way from being able to implement the remedies that would repair our relationship with my parents. First, we had to determine how deep our wounds were and how much healing was required.

People began to notice that something was amiss. Bloggers, tabloids, and social media users had noticed that Derick and I hadn't appeared in any images released by the family in months. The more we remained hidden, the more rumours circulated. It didn't help that TLC never aired our exit interviews, and there was no notification about our departure. People thought that we had just left the show without using any of the exit interview material. Some individuals claimed we had been sacked from the show. Others claimed it was entirely due to Derick's Twitter statements. One thread I saw was about how Derick had clearly ordered me to start wearing pants since Jinger had received so much attention for it, and Derick was desperate to get noticed.

It was all ludicrous, and Derick and I could easily dismiss it. For Pops, however, the situation was different. Anything that harmed the program harmed him, so he appeared eager to return to the mediation, to make things right amongst us all, and to bring us back to the Big House, just like old times.

"You can't put a timeline on healing," our therapist remarked when we inquired how long it would be until we could meet with Mom and Pops again. "You'll just have to tell them that we're not sure when you'll be ready. I believe we should focus our energies on our own health right now."

It was sound advice, the type that makes you breathe with relief. Finally, someone was on our side. And after all those years of trying to fit into whatever schedule the program required, I could say no. I could set my own schedule.

In just a few sessions, Ray had shown us how to interact more successfully with Pops. We realised that the extensive letter we wrote over the summer had been completely incorrect. We'd made way too many allegations and hadn't admitted how we felt about it. There was no way Pops could read it without feeling offended.

So, when I texted Pops and Mom about when we'd be ready to meet again, I followed our therapist's instructions. I stated that we needed some time to work on ourselves, apologised for the fact that everything was taking longer than we had intended, and thanked them for their willingness to work with us.

It felt amazing to be empowered like this, and I was willing to wait however long it took for Derick and me to heal. However, there was one issue that we couldn't put on hold indefinitely: money.

When Derick started at Oklahoma State University as a youngster, his parents gave him some excellent advice: apply for every grant and scholarship imaginable. He did precisely what they advised, sending nearly a hundred letters, applications, and essays to various boards, NGOs, and foundations from which he may potentially receive financial aid. Then donations began to pour in, including $20,000 from OSU, nearly $10,000 from the Buck Foundation, and $1,000 from the local Walmart Neighborhood Market. He ended up getting about half of his expenses covered, saving him tens of thousands of dollars throughout the duration of his degree.

Naturally, when Derick enrolled in law school over a decade later, he followed the same strategy. With two children under the age of four at home and a wife who did not work, money was even tighter than before. He needed every grant he could get, so he started applying.

It didn't take long for him to discover that the money Pops' accountant had declared on my tax forms made it appear that we had far more money than we did. It didn't matter that we had never received the $132,249.98 that had been stated. In terms of trusts and foundations, our tax filings indicated that we did not require significant financial assistance. While that was frustrating, it wasn't our main concern. We were more concerned about what we still didn't know about our finances, the contract, and past taxes with Pops.

Despite all of our progress in treatment and our desire to be on good terms with family and work things out, the email knocked us back a long way. It felt cool. It felt awful. It hurt. Pops appeared to be less giving than we had previously imagined. He was demonstrating Proverbs 23:1-8 in action.

Pops was clearly considering the expense of bringing me into the world, and he was determined to oppose our pleas. We couldn't simply continue the cat-and-mouse game. We were already emotionally exhausted, and we realised that if we didn't act to protect ourselves and improve the situation, things would only become worse. We couldn't continue to live like this forever, so we resolved to take action.

In late October, we engaged an attorney, who sent Pops a formal demand letter requesting the 2014 contract as well as copies of the Mad Family Inc. bylaws, minutes, and other information that I, as a shareholder, should have received already.

Pops went crazy.

He started with the phone. Every day, we received texts, voicemails, and phone calls, but he never responded to our questions. Instead, he was urging us to overcome issues, move on, and work things out. We told him that we, too, wanted to do that, and that all he had to do was contact our attorney and provide the needed information.

He did not.

Then came the next wave, a collaborative effort by several of my siblings. They hit the phones all day, leaving voicemails and texts pleading with us to address this. When that didn't work, several of my siblings began to visit. They'd want to spend hours discussing it, trying to figure out what the problem was and why we weren't doing what Pops wanted. I felt responsible to at least hear them out and demonstrate that we cared by listening. I could just about handle the daytime visits, but when they wanted to talk with Derrick and me until midnight, and Derick had law school exams the next day, we eventually said no.

"What? "How come you won't talk?" they would ask. "This is way more important than law school."

We could see what was happening. Early in 2017, Pops began paying small, non-negotiable amounts per episode to those filming, including spouses and siblings. It appeared to me that they had been misled into thinking they owed nothing and that the $80,000 payout was really generous. That they should be nothing but grateful for all the blessings and good fortune he was bestowing upon them. There were some strings connected, such as needing to pile on Derick and me when we caused trouble, but it appeared that almost none of them were ready to criticise Pops' actions. They were still so afraid of causing dissension among the brethren that they agreed to almost anything.

However, not all visits were intended to apply pressure. One of my siblings came alone and explained what was going on.

"Pops is telling everyone that if we don't stand up to you both on this, we're up against him. He stated that none of us can remain impartial in this situation, as it affects all of us. He claims we might all be sued as a result of what you're doing."

I cried after my sibling went. Pops was angry at Derick and me, but how could he justify involving his other children in this way? How could he mislead them into believing they may be sued when he was fully aware that we were dealing with the Mad Family Inc. corporation rather than our siblings? I felt sad for him. It made me afraid for them.

Our attorney advised us to be patient and ride it out, politely repeating our demands when Pops refused to cooperate. For him, it was routine legal work, but for me, it was a nightmare.

I wasn't coping well. Every time my phone screen displayed a Duggar family name, I would have a fear-induced adrenaline rush. Every tap on the door seemed like we were back in El Salvador, with armed gangs stalking about.

Around the end of November, another of my siblings paid us a visit. For once, there was nothing to say.

"Here," they said, handing over a piece of paper. "Pops says you've got twenty-four hours."

Derick and I studied the paper after my sibling had left. Pops was still attempting to strike a deal with us outside of our formal request for only the Mad Family documents and contract. It was the same deal we had witnessed before. He wanted to pay us $20,000 that day and have us sign an NDA that prohibited us from discussing any of it. We had no intention of signing it.

Our attorney maintained our requests as he communicated with Pops and his CPA via email. As the time for turning over the documents approached, we began discussing the next step—possibly obtaining a court order to obtain the release of the documents we sought.

"Will it work?" I asked Derick. "Do you think he will give us what we are asking for?"

"Yeah. I don't think he'll let it get that far."

It was late, the boys were sleeping, and I was feeling cold. However, my shivering had nothing to do with the weather. It was pure terror.

"How do you know?"

"Because what we are asking for is very reasonable. Because we have a right to them, and it makes sense to anyone with an objective mind, including a judge or jury." Derick exhaled. "Because Pops values the show and wouldn't want all of this to be public and jeopardise the show."

For months, I'd tried to contain my anxiety and despair. Except for our therapist, I had no one to talk to about it, and therapy sessions were sometimes like leaping into a cold lake. We'd be discussing some of Pops' recent issues and how they linked to aspects of my upbringing, and all the blood would be rushing into my ears. My thoughts would spiral so badly that I'd only remember those meetings with Ray as a dream.

I felt myself disintegrating. All of my edges were tattered. I'd spent my entire life with my family. IBLP has emphasised the need of prioritising immediate core family relationships over interactions with others, so some people continue to identify them as immediate and prioritise them over all relationships well into marriage. Now, most of them were against me. I wasn't built for this. I'd gone through stress and trauma before, some of it caused by people in my family, but I'd always been able to rely on others for assistance. They had been my gravity, the force I never had to question and could always count on. But suddenly it felt as if they were gone. Some were still present, but it was different and farther away than previously. They had no idea how to manage it either. Despite having my own great family of four, I felt alone. I have no framework for coping with that.

I awoke one night to the sound of our storm door being opened. Someone began knocking on the door. It was 12:15 a.m.

My heart was instantly pounding in my chest. I was freaking out and reached for Derick. He was sluggish at first, but when the doorbell rang, he jumped out of bed.

"Wait!" I snarled as he left the room.

"Who is it?" Are they really breaking in?

I was at the window. I couldn't see anyone out there, but there was a car on the street. An automobile I recognized.

"It's Mom's car," I explained. "And…"

Whoever had been hammering and knocking on the door gave up, turned around, and returned to the automobile. It was Mom. She'd never done anything like that before, and no one in my family had, so I stared out the window at her, motionless.

I saw her leave.

The adrenaline took hours to leave my body.

Chapter 8: Real. Not Fake

I knew nothing about cocktails, but even from the first sweet sip I could tell that the piña colada was a good one. It was September 2020, a late summer date night for Derick and me, and everything always tasted better when it was just the two of us, sitting side by side in a booth, sharing stories about the boys, sketching future plans like we had on the back porch of our house in El Salvador. But this night, just like this piña colada, was special. It felt like a night to celebrate.

Israel had just started school. Sending your firstborn off on day one is a big enough milestone for every parent, but for me, it felt even more significant. Homeschooling was at the very heart of what IBLP stood for, and they loved quoting Proverbs 22:6 ("Train up a child in the way he should go: and when he is old, he will not depart from it"). It was a nonnegotiable for any true IBLP member, and it was one of the things that first attracted my parents to Mr. Gothard's teaching. And their homeschooling conferences, resources, and training continued to be a big part of the IBLP business model. As a result, not one of my siblings or any of their children had been sent to a public school. I'd been brought up to view the public school system as dangerous and ungodly, and to view anyone who didn't choose to homeschool their kids as an uninformed or risky parent.

Our decision to enrol in Israel in public school represented a significant step on my own journey out from IBLP—an organisation that I was finally able to see clearly. It was a cult, thriving on a culture of fear and manipulation. Derick—who was a perfect example of how a godly man can thrive in public school—helped challenge my thinking. The more we had talked and prayed about sending Israel to public school, the clearer the issue became for me: IBLP had put a lot more energy into teaching me to fear the world beyond its doors than it had put into teaching me to trust God and discern for myself how to reach a good and wise decision on any given issue.

I guess that was why I didn't move the piña colada out of the shot when Derick took a photo of us at the end of the meal. I was going to. When he reached for his phone, I reached out a hand to move the half-empty glass, but then I stopped. Derick had drunk a beer and I'd had my cocktail. It was a special kid-free date time, just the two of us. So, I left it where it was on the table. In the shot. There for everyone to see when I posted the photo later on. I didn't want to be fake. I wanted to be real.

The whole piña colada picture got some people upset. The story—such as it was—got picked up by People magazine and others, but it wasn't anything like the nose ring or the time I started wearing pants. It must have triggered one of Pops' Google alerts, but there was no communication from him. I guess he had gotten the hint a few months earlier when he read online that Derick had been seen drinking a beer. Pops had made contact soon after and offered to send Derick to the same rehab facility Josh had been to, in the hope of curing Derick's clearly raging alcoholism. Since he'd never been drunk or ever had more than two beers in any one sitting, Derick declined.

My desire to be genuine had been growing steadily within me for a long time. Two months had passed since I'd walked out of the attorney's office with the first check for the money declared to the IRS. Pops had left me in no doubt that by pushing him to pay the money we believed we were owed, I wouldn't just be stepping away from Mad Family Inc. I would be placing a large barrier between me and the rest of the Duggar family, and giving Pops control of the narrative my siblings would likely hear. It was daunting, but I knew that Derick and I had made the right decision. And in the year and a half that followed, my journey toward acknowledging and embracing my real self had gathered pace.

At first, things were tough. But for every moment where I felt a sense of relief at getting out of Pops' control, there were a dozen more times when the fear and the guilt felt just as dangerous and painful as they had ever been. We'd left the show, we'd cut the rope that bound us tight to the family, so by rights we should have felt at liberty to make new, deep friendships with people. But all I felt was worried. There were days when I felt more alone than ever. I'd recently read the book Boundaries by Dr. Henry Cloud and Dr. John Townsend and found it very helpful, validating, and encouraging.

Things had gotten worse in April 2019 when Pops sent me a text that included the words "please don't come over when I am not at home." We had already started to feel uncomfortable hanging out at the Big House—sometimes it felt like we'd have to get the courage up before hanging out with some of my family members in any setting. Even Derick was starting to feel the pressure, which manifested itself in the form of an all-out panic attack around Easter time. Being effectively banned from the Big House felt like a reactionary and cruel blow.

Yet in the middle of those dark times, one thing we never failed to be grateful for was the chance to continue seeing Ray for counselling every week. He was a voice of calm in the storm, a steady, unchanging presence when everything else was in a state of decay. Thanks to him I learned a lot about myself, especially when it came to the issue of trusting people. Pops had always warned us about talking to people outside the family—and even advising us against speaking to those inside the family at times—so I'd always found it difficult to be honest with people about things I was struggling with. I was hardwired to be wary, and after everything that happened with In Touch magazine and the story of Josh's abuse, I found it almost impossible to open up to people.

"Have you heard of the word 'attunement'?" Ray asked us one session. Derick and I both looked blank, so he went on to explain about the importance of couples learning to communicate with each other on a deep, emotional level—becoming attuned. Instinctively I liked it, and Derick and I added the word to our vocabulary. We needed it. Somehow, throughout all the chaos around the show and with my family, we'd stayed strong together. We'd been united through all the turmoil, but we still needed help. By introducing this idea of us being attuned to each other, Ray helped us to communicate on a deeper level than we'd been on before.

He knew how to challenge us, encouraging us to talk with others. He advised us to pick a small circle of close friends who we trusted and start talking with them. He also gave us better tools to help us open the lines of communication with my family.

For our homework for one week he said we should draw a target. "Write the names of friends and family inside different rings of the target with the middle being your closest, most trusted relationships, to the widest being the more distant ones. This exercise will help you visualise your relationships, and it's okay if it takes a while to figure out. Those relationships will change at different points in your life, and that's okay too."

It was harder than I thought, and I almost felt guilty not putting all of my family in the inner circle. But it brought clarity and was a helpful, practical step for us as a couple to verbalise and decide which relationships we felt safest in and in which ones we needed healthier boundaries.

"Take a risk," Ray told us when we discussed next week's exercise. He advised us to cultivate close friendships and talk with some of my siblings about problems we'd faced. "If you can share a little bit more about the things you're struggling with, it gives them permission to do likewise."

It wasn't easy. After so many years of being warned not to "stir up contention among the brethren," I was preprogrammed to keep my thoughts to myself. But as soon as I opened up for the first time— saying yes to one of my brothers when he told me he liked a girl and asked if he could come over and get my advice on how he should navigate the relationship without Pops taking control—I realised two amazing things. First, maybe the act of talking about the tough journey that we'd been on could actually be of help to some of the people I loved most and help them avoid some of the same problems we'd faced. Second, when I did talk about it, the sky didn't fall in. And just like drinking a piña colada on a date with my husband, God wasn't angry with me. Muscle memory told me I was sinning, but common sense, long and deep conversations with Derick, as well as my own Bible study, prayer life, and conversations with other Christians told me that I was actually okay. It felt strange, but at twenty-seven years old, I was finally learning to build healthy relationships and have a healthier, less fear driven view of God. And I was realising it was a whole lot harder to "walk the straight and narrow" Christian road and live with balance than to fall to extremes.

So much of my faith has been shaken over the years, but never more so than when things were so painful with Mom and Pops. It was hard to process everything, hard to pick through everything that I had been taught—both at home and in church—and filter truth from lies. At times it was tempting to throw it all out and run away, but even that terrified me. Growing up I'd heard so many horror stories of people who had become "backsliders" or had "lowered their standards" that just the thought of looking critically at my faith felt dangerous and foreign to me.

Deep down I knew that I didn't want to bail on my faith. I was aware that people had used the Bible to manipulate me and press on the nerve of my guilt in order to make me conform to what they felt was acceptable, but I didn't hold that against God.

Talking deeply and honestly felt like a challenge, but it was nothing compared with what had happened that summer. Six months had passed since Pops had given in and paid out that first payment, and I'd not seen him since then. But in June, Grandma Duggar died. She had been a force of nature, and her passing was going to leave a mighty hole in everyone's life, especially Pops. My heart went out to him. For all the disagreement and pain that passed between us—for all the lack of attunement—I felt for him.

When we got the date for Grandma Duggar's funeral, I talked about what I should do with Ray. I had no idea how to navigate it, though I knew for sure that I wanted to go.

"Your dad's going to be hurting," he said. "Seek him out. Go up to him as soon as you can. Don't wait around anxiously for him to come to you. Go straight up and show him that you care."

My throat was dry and my insides were empty as I headed for Tontitown a few days before the funeral. It was only a couple of months after Pops had told me not to go to the Big House when he wasn't there, and it was strange to be feeling so nervous as I pulled down the long gravel drive to the house I had called home for nearly eight years—a house I had helped build. I felt like a visitor, an imposter, and a prodigal all rolled into one. I saw Pops coming out of the house shortly after I parked, and I did what our therapist had suggested and went straight to him.

"I'm so sorry about grandma. I'm sure you must be heartbroken," I said, repeating the words I'd rehearsed in my mind over and over.

Then I gave him a hug. I hadn't rehearsed that, but it wasn't anything I could stop. It just felt right.

"Thank you," he said.

For the first time in years, I felt connected to Pops.

Days later, after the funeral, Derick and I were invited back to the Big House. It was nice to be asked, and I'm sure that Sweet Jilly Muffin would have said yes, but her voice wasn't as loud within me anymore. So I said no. I needed to go home and grieve alone.

For Grandma Duggar.

For everything.

I didn't think that a hug with Pops would change anything overnight, but I appreciated it all the same. And as summer rolled on, things did begin to shift. Pops still didn't want me going over to the Big House unless he was there, but he did start inviting Derick, the boys, and I along to more family events from time to time, sometimes even pressuring us to show up. Most of the events that we were invited to attend didn't include any cameras, which was fine, though I was tempted to wonder if Pops was partly doing it so that he could post pictures of us and squash the rumours that were circulating online about us splitting from the family. I didn't dwell on it. I liked spending time with my family, even if it was hard at times. It felt right. I guess it felt right to Pops too, because just before Thanksgiving, the Big House ban was lifted—partially. Mom told us that we were welcome around the Big House anytime, though Pops added a condition, "as long as you are not only coming over when I am not there." It was a subtle change, and I guess he wanted to make sure that we weren't trying to avoid him too much.

Derick and I were still seeing Ray, so there were plenty more opportunities to reflect and try to make sense of the legacy of growing up like I did. With Derick in law school, and our schedule busy, we tried to be intentional about where we got involved in our church and how we continued building new relationships with people. We started volunteering in the kids' ministry on Sunday mornings to be part of the classes our kids were in and make friends with other parents. It was all hands on deck in the chaos of the kids' church, and there really wasn't much opportunity for anyone to ask about my family.

We were in a kids' church meeting one day in November when my phone started blowing up. I could feel it announcing a new text message every minute or so, and when I snuck a look, I saw that they were all around the same theme—something had happened with my family and people were reaching out to tell me they were praying for us.

As soon as our meeting was over, I checked Google and saw that Homeland Security had raided Josh's car lot. Details were scarce and vague, but it was something to do with an investigation. Later that evening, I saw a statement from Pops too, telling the world that nothing was going on and nobody in the family was being investigated. I hated to think it, but the conflicting details led me to believe that he wasn't telling the whole story. I prayed I was wrong.

Once we made it home and got the kids in bed, I talked to one of my siblings who had just been in on things at the Big House.

"That's not all," they said when I asked them about Pops' statement. "He just called a family meeting. Told us Josh was being investigated. He said they took a bunch of hard drives but that it might all be a setup. So he's telling us to pray that this all comes to an end real quick, and reminds us not to make any statements to anyone."

I could imagine the scene. The heavy silence, everyone wondering what was really going on, but nobody asking their questions out loud. All eyes on Pops, standing in the middle, rallying the troops. Mom sat quietly to the side, looking weary. Like she'd been here too many times already.

For weeks, online rumours danced like a campfire. I stayed away from the gossip, but I was aware that some people were saying that since it was Homeland Security investigating, it must have been an immigration issue. Maybe, I thought. But unlikely.

Mostly I tried to ignore it all. I was grateful for the distance between me and the show, grateful that I wouldn't be called upon to do my bit to defend Pops' other baby. But I felt for my siblings. I worried about them feeling the pressure to help Pops out.

Whatever the investigation into Josh was really about, it had kind of died down by the time 2020 began, and especially by the time Covid hit. As the world shut down and governments told people to retreat to their homes, I knew that—figuratively at least—I was done with hiding. I wanted to connect with people, to take a risk and begin to open up.

By late summer of 2020, Covid was still a risk, but I was grateful for the protocols our local public school district had in place to create a healthy environment for the kids to still be able to attend school safely.

So those first few days, as I prayed over Israel and kissed him goodbye and watched him run into kindergarten, I was thankful. Thankful for God's direction and my husband's wisdom and support as we prayerfully made decisions together as a couple that were best for our family. And though I wasn't terrified of sending Israel into public school, I'd be lying if I said I wasn't at least a little nervous.

Maybe that's why the date night piña colada tasted so good. It wasn't just Israel starting a whole new chapter in his life.

I was too.

Being involved in reality TV does strange things to your relationships. It almost denies you the right to choose who is close to you and who isn't—in the way that our therapist challenged us to do with his exercise. There are times when it seems that everyone feels entitled to be in your inner circle, with full access to your life. It also leaves you in a catch-22. After years of having to share almost every aspect of your life with a show, you crave privacy. If you keep quiet and try to hide away, people just spread more lies and rumours about you. If you defend yourself and try to set the record straight, you will be criticised and deemed to be unworthy of privacy.

It's an impossible choice, and there's no pain-free alternative.

For Derick and me, the truth was important. We've always understood that some individuals will dislike everything we say, do, or believe, regardless of the facts. We cannot change them, and we must accept that. But everyone deserves to know and share the truth.

We both recognized that there was more to being authentic than posting images on Instagram, and we wanted to go beyond leaving a few clues and hoping that people would figure it out for themselves. We wanted to put our therapist's advice into action, so after some thinking, we decided in October 2020 to film a video of the two of us discussing where we were at on a few issues. It was low-key, with just Derick and me sitting on the couch, my phone balanced on a stack of books on the coffee table. We put it up as a Q&A session and worked through a variety of questions. Why did we leave the show? Has there been any distance with the family, and why? Do you notice a difference in yourself since you began therapy? It was difficult and unpleasant at times, but being honest with others felt good.

We uploaded it and waited for a reaction.

Viewers gave warm and supportive comments. People magazine picked up the story, and we had an interview with them. But the response I was most interested in was Mom and Pop's.

They made no comment at all.

We felt relieved.

On Friday, March 5, 2021, Derick was at home completing remote learning. Israel was at school, and I was reading to Samuel and working on other projects when we heard a tap on the door. Two men stood there. One is in his late thirties, and the other is in his mid-forties. Both wore dark collared shirts. Both seemed serious.

"Jill Dillard?"

"Yes."

"We are from Homeland Security. Can we ask you some questions about your brother, Josh Duggar?

I told them I'd like my husband to be able to speak with them as well, but he was occupied right now. So I took their card and vowed to call back to set up a time.

Three days later, they returned as agreed. At first, the queries focused on Josh's business, his car lot, who worked with him, and so on. I did my best, but I knew almost nothing about his automobile. I'd driven past it several times before, but I don't recall ever visiting him there.

"I'm sorry I can't be more helpful," I replied.

There was a pause. Afterward, "What about the abuse incident?"

"I don't want to talk about that," I muttered.

"Why?"

It was my turn to take a pause. It's time to be real. "I believe there are two possible reasons. One, because we have a pending lawsuit about all of this. Second, I just don't want to go there. I'm sorry, but that's the way things are.

When the In Touch story was published in 2015, my encounter with the paparazzi left me scared and panicked. It took years before the wounds began to heal. I still couldn't relax at home without obsessively scrutinising every automobile parked on the street outside. They kept coming. And they would always try to connect the prior abuse to their stories, reinforcing my pain. Every year or so, just when I thought I'd grown used to life without them, they'd appear, waiting outside the house when I returned home, and following me throughout town. They once took a picture of Derick when he returned from a run, and it ended up accompanying the narrative "Disgraced Derick seemed to have a lot of time on his hands after getting sacked from Counting On.

I suppose I should have seen this coming. With Josh's inquiry ongoing, the paparazzi were destined to return.

It happened a month after Derick and I spoke with the Homeland Security officers. Derick was gone at the time, and I was at home with the boys. Someone rang the doorbell, and I figured it was for a delivery.

I knew right away when I saw him standing on the doorstep. The travel-creased clothes, the phoney smile that failed to reach his ragged eyes. But there was no camera that I could see.

"'Ello Jill," he said with a heavy London accent. "I am from the Sun." Do you know your bruvver is about to get arrested? "Any comments?"

I was polite but said, "Sorry, no comment," before closing the door. I then tried to recall how to breathe.

Josh was arrested three days later. From that point forward, I felt like I'd been thrown into a hurricane.

Within hours, one of the Homeland Security personnel contacted me to inform me that they were providing my full interview to the defence. They were forced to do it, but I detested it all the same. I was getting drawn back into the drama, and I felt powerless to stop it.

A week after Josh's arrest, Derick and I watched his detention hearing online. Derick assured me it would last one hour. Instead, it took six. We learnt a lot that day about Josh's allegations, which included downloading child sexual assault material. These charges were far more serious than I had anticipated, and I was astounded to learn how horrific the atrocities he was accused of were. And when a Homeland Security agent testified about the day they searched Josh's vehicle lot, I was surprised by Josh's early emotions about the raid. He appeared uneasy, even asking, "What is this about?" Has anyone been downloading child pornography?

Unsurprisingly, TLC cancelled the show again, and this time there was no high-profile exclusive interview to help it get back on track. The Duggars' stint as a filming family was finally finished.

I tried to stay focused on the boys and not let Josh's situation make me feel uncomfortable or frantic again. It wasn't easy, but all the time Derick and I had spent in therapy helped. I told myself several times that this was not a replay of the original investigation or the In Touch piece. It wasn't easy because there was a media frenzy around every stage of Josh's court proceedings, and the earlier In Touch article was mentioned in almost every story. But I could make my own decisions. I didn't have to be involved in the family drama anymore.

In August, I discovered that wasn't quite accurate. Over five years had passed since my sisters and I filed our case against the City of

Springdale, Arkansas; Washington County, Arkansas; Kathy O'Kelley; Ernest Cate; Rick Hoyt; In Touch magazine, and its parent company Bauer. The defendants had tried their hardest to slow things down over the years. But things were coming to an end. We were informed that a court date had been scheduled for December, and as a result, my sisters and I, along with several of our husbands, were required to give our depositions.

I felt afraid. Knowing that I was going to be questioned by lawyers for hours and give my account of what had happened brought back memories of some of my most anxious moments—El Salvador, Megyn Kelly, and the original investigation, when I was afraid that one wrong word from me would result in us all being taken away from Mom and Pops.

In the days preceding up to my deposition, I couldn't concentrate, eat without nausea, or sleep without having nightmares. Getting out of bed was too much. My gut felt as if it had been tightly encircled with razor wire. For years, I had tried to bury so much of my anguish. I believed I had dealt with it. But now it was back, and it was scarier than ever.

My deposition took seven hours. Every second felt like torment.

When it got to the point where I thought I would shout, I excused myself and went to the restroom. I attempted to get rid of the terror and misery, but all I could do was dry heave over the toilet and cry into a pillow.

When it was over, I hugged the boys and cried in Derick's arms until the room was completely black.

Then, in September, we discovered we were pregnant. After everything that had transpired with Samuel's delivery, I had no idea if I would ever be able to conceive again, but there it was: the clear pink line on the test. I was so thrilled that I was able to suppress the emotions that the deposition had triggered. Yet the following month, I miscarried. It struck me hard. As I mourned the loss of tiny River Bliss Dillard, I was asking big questions about whether I'd ever have another child. A part of me accepted that if my body couldn't carry another baby to term, so be it. I already had two lovely, healthy boys, so it was simple to be thankful. But I knew what I wanted: more babies. I had consulted health doctors and received a regimen for treating any probable pregnancy, but I wasn't finished yet. The longing hovered over me like a shadow. I wasn't sure what to do with it.

Pops had to be in court before Josh's trial began. I wasn't there, but Derick learned about it from a family acquaintance and told me it didn't go well. Pops appeared terrified and aggressive, indignantly demanding the judge, "Are you going to let this happen?" After being asked a question he didn't want to answer about past abuse and information disclosure. It had not gone well, and Pops had earned a warning from the judge—who happened to be the same guy who was due to hear the case that my sisters and I were presenting.

It wasn't a good beginning.

Then, in November, just as I was getting ready for Josh's jury trial, something unexpected happened. We became pregnant again.

I was on the prosecution's witness list, therefore I was advised to avoid reading about the trial. It was not easy. Josh's slow fall from grace made global headlines, and at times it seemed like nothing else was happening in the world. Derick told me that there were paparazzi outside the courtroom and the Big House. The days were long, but I was grateful to be spending them peacefully at home, with my blinds closed just in case cameras showed up, hanging out with my boys and praying for the health of the new life growing inside me.

At other moments, I thought about Josh. I'd been told that I could be called at any time and expected to testify against him in court the next day. That was a sobering thought—and a little unnerving at times—but I was willing to try it. I had considered what Josh had done and reached a clear conclusion. After years of following the family line and believing Pops when he stated things were better handled within the family, I wanted something new to happen. I wanted to know the truth. I wanted the evidence to come out. And I wanted Josh to be incarcerated for an extended period of time.

I was furious at what he had done. He had harmed innocent youngsters with his deeds and then continued to dodge responsibility.

I, too, felt sorry. unhappy that Josh had turned into such a monster, unhappy that despite all the opportunities to reform, he had squandered them as he continued down a dark, dreadful path. Like the rest of the world, I was finally able to see my elder brother for who he was: a man unable to control himself, completely removed from the reality of how much he was hurting people.

The more I reflected, the more I realised how much I missed my carefree childhood. We used to run around and play, plucking fruit from the trees in our yard. Back then, there were only eight of us kids, and our small garden felt like Eden. But, like the previous paradise, sin crept in. Evil has spread. The innocence was broken.

The trial brought back everything from the past, including news stories about the abuse. I was troubled by this, humiliated as before. But things were different this time. I had a stronger network of friends. I was learning how to be vulnerable with them about my family, and I knew that for my own mental health, I couldn't live in seclusion this time. And, for the first time, I felt tremendously supported.

Friends checked in on me and told me they were praying. They provided coffee or ordered meals for my family when I was exhausted from my pregnancy and lacked the energy to do anything. It didn't solve the difficulties, but it gave me the strength to keep going.

And it was not only my buddies. Several of my siblings began to contact me. For the first time, it was evident that some of them were growing sceptical of the story they'd been hearing at home. As they observed the Duggar family show, they began to raise their own questions.

I hated having to go through such a difficult experience again, and I hated that it had pulled in my entire extended family, but I was grateful that I could look back and see the progress, the positive changes in some parts of my relationships and in myself. And that gave me new hope for the future.

Toward the end of the trial, I was advised that I would no longer be required to testify. The prosecution had provided everything they needed to present, thus my testimony was no longer required. I sighed with relief. Probably sobbed a little too, especially when Derick returned home from the trial that night.

"What are you going to do?" he inquired. Being off the witness list allowed me to enter the court. "Are you going to come?"

I debated it for a while before deciding.

It was nearly impossible to tell the difference between pregnancy and anxious nausea, and when I stepped into the courtroom and sat quietly on the bench opposite Derick, I had to take a moment to collect my breath and keep my mind from racing.

When I was able to glance up, I realised how odd everything seemed.

Josh sat with his legal team, as if he were facing no more serious charges than a parking penalty.

There were Pops, Jessa, Joy and her husband, Austin, Jason, Justin and his wife, Claire, and Josh's wife, Anna. They all looked like they were at a funeral. They were pallid. Exhausted. Beaten.

Then there came the media, who outnumbered everyone else. They were keeping an eye on all of us, observing and evaluating everything we did. I'd never felt so claustrophobic before. I've never felt such a strong desire to run before.

But I did not run. I stayed and listened to both sides' conclusions. More than time, I squeezed Derick's hand. Three from me. Four from him.

Before the new crisis, I had hoped Josh would change, or at least desire to change.

But as the reality about his behaviour became clear, I became concerned about who else might be harmed if he was permitted to continue his life as usual. It became more evident that prison was the safest place for Josh and others around him.

Previously, he had apologised for viewing adult content. He appeared to be less sorry as he descended into deeper and worse misdeeds. He never admitted his most recent offences, nor did he demonstrate guilt or remorse. Perhaps he was worried this time about the very real consequences that awaited him. I do not know.

But the entire experience made me feel ill to my core.

I decided against returning to court the next—and final—day. I'd seen enough in one day, heard enough proof, and spoken with enough people to feel no need to return. Besides, I was fatigued and didn't want to do anything that may endanger the baby.

But Derick was present for the ruling. He contacted me shortly after the verdict was issued.

"They found him guilty," he added, but I had been following the news on my phone and already knew.

For a second, I wasn't sure what to say. After so many words, secrets, and falsehoods, it was difficult to put my feelings into syllables. At the end, all I could say was, "I think they got it right."

Later, Derick and I sat at a laptop and began typing. We wanted to post a statement on our family blog quickly.

I knew precisely how I wanted it to begin, and Derick watched me type.

Today was a challenging day for our family.

Our hearts go out to the victims of child abuse and exploitation.

Following that, I struck a block. I tried a couple different lines, but they all appeared incorrect on the screen.

"What do you want people to know?" Derick asked.

I closed my eyes.

"We've been lied to so much. But now, we finally found out the truth.

The contents of this book may not be copied, reproduced or transmitted without the express written permission of the author or publisher. Under no circumstances will the publisher or author be responsible or liable for any damages, compensation or monetary loss arising from the information contained in this book, whether directly or indirectly. .

Disclaimer Notice:

Although the author and publisher have made every effort to ensure the accuracy and completeness of the content, they do not, however, make any representations or warranties as to the accuracy, completeness, or reliability of the content. , suitability or availability of the information, products, services or related graphics contained in the book for any purpose. Readers are solely responsible for their use of the information contained in this book

Every effort has been made to make this book possible. If any omission or error has occurred unintentionally, the author and publisher will be happy to acknowledge it in upcoming versions.

Printed in Great Britain
by Amazon

54136447R00076